Managing Anxiety Using Mindfulness based Cognitive Therapy

Managing Anxiety Using Mindfulness based Cognitive Therapy

Matt Broadway-Horner

CBT in the City Series: Over thinking In Anxiety

Book Cover and illustrations are by WPN De Silva Pradeep@imaginemagazines.com

ISBN: 151425588X
ISBN-13: 9781514255889

Quick Look at Contents

Introduction · xxi

Phase One. **First Leg of the Journey:
        Getting Started with Managing Anxiety** · · · · · · · · · · · · · **1**

Chapter 1 Introducing Anxiety and the Mindfulness Remedy · · · · · · · · 3

Chapter 2 Challenging Your Anxiety · 30

Phase Two. **Second Leg of the Journey:
        Getting to the Crux of Your Anxiety** · · · · · · · · · · · · · · · **39**

Chapter 3 Becoming More Mindful · 41

Chapter 4 Understanding the Brain and Thought Processes · · · · · · · · 53

Chapter 5 Examining Your Emotions · 64

Chapter 6 Getting Motivated and Improving Self-Esteem · · · · · · · · · 82

Phase Three. **Penultimate Part of the Journey:
        Moving On and Maintaining Gains** · · · · · · · · · · · · · · **101**

Chapter 7 Techniques for Changing and Moving Forward · · · · · · · · 103

Chapter 8 Taking Your Next Steps and Going Beyond · · · · · · · · · · · · 114

Chapter 9 Reducing Your Chance of Relapse · · · · · · · · · · · · · · · · · 128

Phase Four. **Finishing Your Journey:**
        Reenergise on Some Nourishing Facts · · · · · · · · · · · · **133**

Chapter 10 Ten Tips for Tackling Anxiety · · · · · · · · · · · · · · · · · · 135

Chapter 11 Ten Mindful Attitudes for Easing Self-Critical Thoughts · · 141

Chapter 12 Ten Mindful Resources for Managing Anxiety · · · · · · · · · 148

Chapter 13 Ten Tips for Challenging Distorted Thinking · · · · · · · · · · 153

Appendices · 165

Index · 175

Table of Contents

Introduction · xxi

About This Book · xxiii

CBT in the City Series Structure · xxv

Phase One. **First Leg of the Journey:**
Getting Started with Managing Anxiety · · · · · · · · · · · · · 1

Chapter 1   Introducing Anxiety and the Mindfulness Remedy · · · · · · · · 3

Exploring the Anxiety Warehouse · 3

Uncovering Common Causes of Anxiety · · · · · · · · · · · · · · · 6

Identifying What Fuels Anxiety · 8

A Brief Look at the Emotions That Occur
Alongside Anxiety · 10

Emotional Responsibility · 17

Making Sense of the Symptoms · 18

Appetite Changes · 19

Feelings of Being Punished and Other
Common Thoughts· 20

Let's Take a Step Back and See If the Life You
Have Now Has Shrunk· 21

Filling the Void with Junk· 21

Inability to Concentrate · 22

Irritability· 23

Lacking Pleasure and Enjoyment in Things· · · · · · · · · · · · · 23

Low Mood · 24

Seeking Isolation from Other People · · · · · · · · · · · · · · · · · · 24

Self-Harm · 25

Sex Drive · 25

Thoughts of Suicide · 26

Starting Out on Your Journey into Mindfulness · · · · · · · · 27

Introducing the Basic Principles of Mindfulness · · · · · · · · 27

Walking the Path of Self-Discovery · · · · · · · · · · · · · · · · · · · 28

Thriving by Doing Less and Noticing More · · · · · · · · · · · · 28

Moving from Anxiety towards Mindful Well-Being· · · · · · 28

Chapter 2   Challenging Your Anxiety · 30

Entering the Beginner Mind. 30

Wake Up! Realising That You're on Autopilot. 31

Switching On Your Problem-Solving Ability 31

Getting Your Concentration Level Back on Track. 32

Accepting That Too Much Control Is Bad for You 32

Reflecting on Your Ideas for Living 33

Considering How You Would Like to Live or Be
Remembered. 33

As a husband or wife? 34

As a worker? 34

As a parent? 34

As a business owner?. 34

As an artist? 35

Understanding the Life-Shrinkage Model 36

Reengaging and Nurturing the Idea That Life Goes On . . 37

Phase Two. **Second Leg of the Journey: Getting to the
Crux of Your Anxiety** · **39**

Chapter 3   Becoming More Mindful· 41

There Is Nothing Wrong with Thinking and
Having Feelings 41

Don't Take Your Thoughts Personally 44

Discovering the Breath 46

Meditations to Start. 46

    Meditation Using the Eyes 46

    Meditation Using the Mouth 47

    Attention-Training Exercise 47

    Mindfulness of the Breath. 47

    Meditation in Action 47

    Sitting with Sounds. 48

    Sitting with Thoughts and Feelings 48

    Sitting with Choiceless Awareness 48

Who Is Breathing? 48

From Vulnerability Comes Creativity and Personality 49

Cultivating Strength and Smashing Shame 50

Moment by Moment. 50

The Way of Awareness 51

Chapter 4 Understanding the Brain and Thought Processes · · · · · · · · 53

Understanding How Your Brain Makes Decisions. 53

Meeting System One: Your Intuition 54

Meeting System Two: Your Reasoning 55

Using Mindfulness to Help You Look at the
Bigger Picture 55

Do You Have Intruders? Taking Care of
Obsessive Thoughts 57

"Let's Enjoy the Party" as the Way to Recovery. 58

Using Negative Thoughts to Your Advantage 59

You Are Not Your Thoughts—This Isn't a Fusion Thing . . . 61

Beating, Brooding, and Worrying. 61

Recognising Opportunities 62

Taking an Interest in Life 63

Keeping SMART. 63

Chapter 5   Examining Your Emotions · 64

There Are Many Emotions in the Warehouse Called
Anxiety. 65

Exploring Shame 65

Assessing Anger 68

Acknowledging Anxiety. 70

Angry Hurt 72

Looking at Low Mood 73

Chasing Your Tail! 73

Emotions Are Our Friends 75

Noticing, Describing, and Tolerating Your Feelings 75

Stuck in a Cycle of Reacting to Stress Instead of
Responding to It? 76

Take a Look! 76

Change Is a Sure Thing. 77

Listening to Your Body 78

Working with Physical Pain 79

Going on a Journey from Beginner Mind to Wise Mind . . . 80

Chapter 6 Getting Motivated and Improving Self-Esteem · · · · · · · · · 82

Identifying Issues of Low Self-Worth. 83

Wanting High Self-Esteem? 83

Questioning What You Really Want. 84

Avoiding Errors When Challenging Low Self-Worth. 84

Thinking That You're Inferior 84

Feeling Superior 85

Believing That You're Special 85

Trying to Control Other People 85

Seeking Approval 86

Behaving Defensively 86

Being Specific 86

Responding and Not Reacting 86

Knowing Yourself 87

Playing the Rating Game 87

Practicing Unconditional Acceptance 87

Appreciating That Unconditional Self-Acceptance
Is the Key 88

Know That Unconditional Other Acceptance Is the Key . . . 90

Believing That Unconditional Life Acceptance Is the Key . . . 90

Dispassionately viewing Anxiety 90

Be Kind to Yourself 91

The Prejudice Model 93

Taking One Step at a Time—and Being Content 96

Realising That You Don't Have to Be Superhuman. 96

Understanding That It's What You Do Next That Counts . . . 97

Appreciating Your Worth as a Human Being 97

Being Bad Isn't the End of the World! 98

Stepping Back to Take a Good Look 98

Finding Fault with the Concept of Self-Confidence 99

Developing Task Confidence 99

Phase Three. **Penultimate Part of the Journey:
   Moving On and Maintaining Gains** **101**

Chapter 7 Techniques for Changing and Moving Forward · · · · · · · 103

Living Mindfully Day to Day 104

Discovering the New, Healthy You. 104

Detective Columbo, Please Sign Up for Duty! 105

Learning to Be Off Duty. 106

Rediscovering Relationships 107

Learning to Say No. 108

The Crossroad Model 109

Allowing Yourself to Be Happy. 110

Defining Yourself by Your Present 111

Getting Out of Your Comfort Zone 111

Mindfulness Meditations. 112

Chapter 8   Taking Your Next Steps and Going Beyond. 114

Meeting Doctors, Patients, and People 115

Cluing into Long-Term Conditions and Their
Impacts on Depression 117

Dealing with Diabetes. 117

Surveying Strokes 118

Having Knowledge of Heart Problems 119

Being Aware of Bodily Distress. 119

Comprehending Cancer 119

Understanding Multiple Sclerosis. 120

Moving towards a United Perspective on Health 120

Looking at Mind and Body. 121

Working with Physical Pain 121

Getting Familiar with Attitudes That Can Harm
and Heal 122

Going the Way of Awareness 122

Making the Most of New Beginnings. 123

Keeping Up with Mindfulness Practice 123

Role Stress 124

People Stress 124

Work Stress 125

Food Stress 126

World Stress 126

Chapter 9 Reducing Your Chance of Relapse · · · · · · · · · · · · · · · · · 128

Reducing Your Chance of Relapse 128

Discovering the Danger Zones 129

Signposting 129

Using Your Backup 130

Remembering That Practice, Practice, Practice
Makes Permanent 130

Being Kind to Yourself 131

Being in Charge 131

A Final Note: About Medication 132

Phase Four. **Finishing Your Journey:**
Reenergise on Some Nourishing Facts 133

Chapter 10 Ten Tips for Tackling Anxiety. 135

    Enjoy Physical Exercise. 135

    Take Pride in Your Appearance 136

    Take Care of Your Home. 136

    Do Attention-Training Exercises 137

    Draw a Line in the Sand 137

    Be Assertive 138

    Make Attitudes Count. 138

    Commit to Your Choices. 139

    Know That Acceptance Is Not Resignation 139

    The Tourist Exercise 140

Chapter 11 Ten Mindful Attitudes for Easing Self-Critical Thoughts. . 141

    If I Look to the Future, Then I Have No Present 142

    I Would Like Things to Be X, but Life Goes On If Not. . . 142

    I Can Grow and Will Grow 143

    Perfection Stifles Creativity 143

    It's OK to Get It Wrong—You're a Fallible
    Human Being 144

It's Not the End of the World 144

I Can Find My Own Path to Fulfillment 145

It's OK to Love and Be Loved 145

No One Person Has the Full Truth, so Let's Join Forces . 146

It Is In Our Diversity That We Have Our Unity 147

Chapter 12 Ten Mindful Resources for Managing Anxiety · · · · · · · · 148

Doing the Chocolate Twirl Bite Size Chunk 148

Engaging in the Walking Meditation 149

Brushing Your Teeth 150

Noticing the Pleasure in the Small Stuff 150

Keeping in Touch 151

Making Someone Else Happy 151

Offering Forgiveness 151

Allowing 151

Fostering Appreciation 152

Establishing Your Relationship with Yourself 152

Chapter 13 Ten Tips for Challenging Distorted Thinking · · · · · · · · 153

Avoid Catastrophising 153

Step into the Grey. 154

Keep the Dictator in His Place. 154

Think Practically—Not Magically 155

Don't Police Every Thought. 155

Party Like It's 1999! 156

Don't Take Things Personally. 156

Consider Possibilities 157

Know That You're Fallible 157

Remember That Shouting at It Does Not Get Rid of It . . 157

Appendices. 165

Behaviour Activation Form. 167

Cost-Benefit Analysis 168

Formulation of my Beliefs and Rules 169

Ideas for Living Form 170

Positive Data Form 172

Practice of Meditation Form. 173

Index 175

Introduction

Anxiety is one of the most common mental health conditions. It affects one in five. It can accompany other long-term conditions like asthma, diabetes, cancer, strokes, and heart conditions. Yet there is a lot of misunderstanding about anxiety, and it is often confused with other problems.

This book is a guide to understanding anxiety and looks at it honestly—warts and all. Through educating yourself about the common signs and symptoms of anxiety, hopefully you will realise that you are not alone. You will also learn about the typical cycles this illness takes. Mindfulness-Based Cognitive Therapy (MBCT), the treatment this book discusses, is an approach that has been tried and tested. It will help you understand what fuels anxiety, what you can do to recover, and how to stay well longer. It's also an approach that not only helps you, but others in your life, too.

A patient told me once that he had suffered from anxiety for twenty years but had never found anything that could help. He had been on medications throughout that time and even tried psychoanalysis—but still no change as he had been misdiagnosed and he was suffering from Obsessive Complusive Disorder. He decided that was as good as life would get and resigned all hope of getting better. A friend who happened to be a patient of mine eventually recommended Cognitive-Based Therapy (CBT). When he arrived for his initial consultation, he was certainly demoralised. Jumping to the end of the story, some sessions later he was discharged and diagnosed as no longer suffering from OCD. He no longer broods or worries for six hours daily. He has renewed energy and zest for life again. He acknowledged that if his friend had not had therapy, then he would never have known about the good impact of CBT, either. This book is designed to be that good friend for you—and to be easily accessible on your bookshelf or in your handbag or car. MBCT can help you overcome your anxiety as well. This book gathers together practical information and provides tools to get you started using MBCT on your own.

About This Book

My goal is to help you understand anxiety in its many forms. I have made the assumption that this will be your first introduction to Mindfulness-Based Cognitive Therapy. I have tried to keep the language simple and straightforward, and I have tried to limit the amount of jargon used. I have structured the text so that you can dip into it at different points and still come away with useful, actionable information.

First, this book talks about the signs and symptoms of anxiety and looks at what fuels it. Once you understand that, I will introduce you to MBCT treatment. This approach's techniques have proven to be effective at demolishing anxiety. Think of this book as an encouraging friend whom you meet over coffee; it's on your side and empowers you to find your own path of enlightenment.

The book has seven main goals:

- To show you how the basic CBT model defines and treats anxiety
- To reveal the scientific basis behind Mindfulness-Based Cognitive Therapy
- To help you identify how the problems associated with anxiety develop
- To show you how to tap into the "beginner's mind" in MBCT
- To teach you how to demolish anxiety
- To help you move from the "beginner's mind" to your "wise mind" when you're ready
- To help you learn how to prevent anxiety from happening again in the future

CBT in the City
Series Structure

I would like to help you by highlighting smaller headings within the phases. They originally appeared in the early publications of the clinic newsletter called *CBT Monthly* and are well known to the subscribers of the company CBT in the City. These are here to help highlight areas for learning and provide quick access to information:

Pit Stop Exercises
Motto
Top Tip
Pause
Fact Corner
Diagnosis Corner
Psychobabble Defined
Action Ideas
Therapy Made a Difference—The Human Condition
The Day in the Life of a Therapist

The book is broken out into four main sections, or "phases":

Phase One. First Leg of the Journey: Getting Started with Managing Anxiety

The saying "knowledge is power" couldn't be more true for people battling anxiety. This section explores what anxiety is and how it affects us. It details the common signs and symptoms of anxiety and will help you see that you are not alone. This also introduces you to the clinical approaches used to help tackle and overcome anxiety.

Phase Two. Second Leg of the Journey: Getting to the Crux of Your Anxiety

In this section, the emphasis is on introducing techniques you can keep in your toolbox to help you demolish anxiety. It focuses on the triad that fuels anxiety: thoughts, feelings, and behaviors. Once you understand how your thoughts and feelings influence anxiety, you have the knowledge to move on to the next step, which is attacking anxiety from within.

Phase Three. Penultimate Part of the Journey: Moving On and Maintaining Gains

This section looks primarily at how to maintain growth and gains achieved in Phases One and Two. It helps you focus on learning to enjoy your newfound health and on enjoying living life mindfully, in the moment. It also provides a refresher on the original signs of anxiety you may have encountered, unaware, in the past in order to help you know how to combat them in the future.

Phase Four. Finishing Your Journey: Reenergise on Some Nourishing Facts

This is designed to give you quick, easy access to information. Patients have told me that sometimes they struggle at odd hours and want a tip or exercise to help them through those bad and hopeless moments. This section provides you with mindful resources and quick references on how to maintain helpful attitudes, how to tackle self-critical thoughts, and how to challenge distorted thinking.

Moving Forward

It's important that you don't just read this book passively, but that you actually try out the Pit Stop exercises and learn how to use some of the tools it offers. Doing so will most effectively help you demolish your anxiety. I challenge you to take action!

The approaches within the CBT tradition used in this book

Cognitive Therapy

Created by Aaron Beck with his Depression Triad model, looking at the thoughts and assumptions we make about ourselves; about others and the world. These assumptions can be challenged and changed into helpful ones

Rational Therapy

Created by Albert Ellis who looked at rigid attitudes and how they create difficult emotions and self-defeating behaviours. He developed the unconditional self-acceptance theory and the idea of low frustration tolerance. He coined the phrase "Don't be a mustabator!"

Acceptance and Commitment Therapy

Created by Stephen Hayes and looks at our value systems and how this could be the source of our disturbance. Using metaphors and analogies to help you move forward towards your ideas for living thus tapping into the bigger picture of your life

Behaviour Activation 3rd Wave therapies

Created by Skinner initially which formed Behaviour Therapy in the 1960's but later opened up and revived by Lewinsoln and Jacobson in the 1970's. This incorporates cognitions into the process which Skinner did not do as he was unsure what impact this would have. The TRAP and TRAC, Crossroads Model are theories in BA

Mindfulness Based Cognitive Therapy

Created by John Kabat-Zinn who studied the effects of Buddhism and found good effects upon health. It is a self-directed process that understands that we can observe what we notice around and within us. Thoughts, emotions are events to watch and study and by taking a back step helps us to take many steps forward

Compassion Focused Therapy

Created by Prof Paul Gilbert who follows a evolutionary psychological perspective and created theories of how to develop the compassionate mind and that compassionate is the key that opens the door to many problems we experience today

About the Author

Matt Broadway-Horner is a registered psychotherapist, a registered scientist and a registered nurse. He is the director of Clinical and Wellbeing Services at CBT in the City Clinics. He was first trained in CBT during his undergraduate years at St George's, University of London. He later completed his master's degree in CBT at Goldsmiths College, University of London, in 2005. He is currently a PhD candidate with a focus in Psychology. He also has private clinics in Central London, Southgate, and in St Albans, where he treats depression, anxiety, and trauma. For contact please e-mail him at matt@cbtinthecity.com.

He is on the alumni of University of East London, Goldsmiths College-University of London, St Georges-University of London and Kingston University. He is an accredited member of The British Association of Behavioural Cognitive Psychotherapies, Member of Association Of Rational Emotive Behaviour Therapy, Nursing and Midwifery Council, International Association of Cognitive Therapies and Association of Science Education

If you want to subscribe to the clinic's free magazine, please visit www.imaginemagazines.com

For information on day therapy services and executive services, visit www.cbtinthecity.com

For information on Mindfulness-Based Cognitive Therapy, visit www.mindfulnessandthecity.com

- Join our Facebook groups: CBT in the City—CBT in the City for Schools—Mindfulness and the City
- Follow us on Twitter: CBTDaily—SchoolsCBT—MindfulnessCB

Acknowledgments

I would like to thank all those whom I have learned from, both my professional colleagues in the psychotherapy/psychology world and patients. There are too many in both groups to mention here. A huge thank-you to my family and my life partner.

Phase One

FIRST LEG OF THE JOURNEY: GETTING
STARTED WITH MANAGING ANXIETY

CHAPTER 1

Introducing Anxiety and the Mindfulness Remedy

In This Chapter You Will

- Learn to understand the usual cycles of anxiety
- Understand what fuels anxiety
- Learn to take a stand against the "the bully"

Trying to come to grips with anxiety is a huge task, and it requires time. Take it day by day. In this chapter, I will show you the most common signs and symptoms of anxiety and how the skill of reflection can help you make sense of them and, ultimately, move forward. Self-discovery is the main focus here; introspection can provide some ways for you to manage your relationship with yourself and others.

Exploring the Anxiety Warehouse

Think of anxiety as a warehouse. In a warehouse, there are many boxes that hold many different contents; it's the same with anxiety. Anxiety boxes might be worry about the future, shame, anger, low mood, and obsessional brooding, to name a few. Once you see anxiety in this way, you can see why therapists often treat it by focusing on opening up one or two specific boxes at a time. Approaching and treating each contributing factor individually helps you gain confidence that you can eventually open up all the boxes.

Anxiety is usually defined as being one of several problems:

Anxiety: This is the perception of a threat that sets off a chain reaction within the body. This reaction is called "The Fight and Flight mechanism" and is there to keep us safe. It becomes a problem when the anxiety is constant and often because of individual circumstances, making the individual feel controlled or punished by the problem, feeling on edge, "wired" and unable to concentrate with low energy levels.

Panic Attacks: Acute attacks of anxiety that play out in specific moments like being "put on the spot" and believing danger is imminent. The attack is accompanied by palpitations, uneasy breathing, pain in heart, hot and cold clammy skin, brain fog, urination, faecal incontinence and feeling as thou the world has ended. Often signs and symptoms are interpreted as other crisis medical reasons like having a heart attack.

Social Anxiety General: Fear of others and being "under the microscope". Fear of looking and being perceived as stupid, socially inept, boring, weird or freaky. The response is to avoid social gatherings for fear of being misunderstood by their shaking, blushing or sweating in public.

Social Anxiety Specific: Fear of others and being "under the microscope" in intimate situations in small gatherings where personal information is shared. Conference speeches are not a problem for these people as they do not fear the anonymous large gatherings.

Health Anxiety: The individual is convinced beyond a shadow of a doubt that they are suffering from a terminal condition like for instance cancer. They have received numerous medical tests to show and prove medically that they do not have the condition but they still persist to prove the medical experts wrong. They have a feeling that the body is not well often spending thousands of thousands of pounds, even selling their home to find out the problem.

Obsessive Compulsive Disorder: Believing that if they don't carry out an action that they are at fault; blaming themselves for what happens to others. They are compelled to act because if they don't they believe they are "mad, bad or dangerous" if they don't. The most common themes in OCD that keep suffers in silence are mainly in the Bad and dangerous domain; fear of being a paedophile, rapist, murderer, demon possessed, child killer, incest and being gay. In response to these fears they cuts themselves off from partners, children and whole families and communities in order to keep others safe. NB: They are not dangerous at all and need to be re-introduced to family and communities through therapy. Many seek help when the obsession has morphosed into a 3rd or 4th obsession like cleaning and being dirty because it is more socially acceptable to doctors.

Body Dysmorphia Disorder: The belief that beauty is distorted and they they match that of the elephant man. It is a specific area that they have deemed to be so ugly and deformed that they have many suicidal thoughts and will look for ways to end their life

Performance Anxiety: This used to be called 'Stage Fright' which is the phobia of performing in public for fear that they will shake or carry out an involuntary unwanted action. This is common in the acting world as well as schools and job interviews.

Vomit Phobia: Fear of eating certain foods as they might become ill and never recover. They fear that they will take too much time off work and lose their jobs, house and living status. There are specific cases that draw upon the origins to traumatic early child hood experiences of illness. The impact of this in adult life are many and varied but some examples are; loosing teeth, unable to hold a long lasting relationships, avoiding social situations, low body weight (often misunderstood as an eating disorder), unhealthy lifestyle due to eating one food item only.

Phobias: Acute fear of objects like needle, birds, spiders etc that lead to avoiding situations to keep themselves safe. Fears can be passed down to children and can see the stories, customs and myths passed through generations. Others phobias include, vomit and fainting. Many experience constant fainting which disables them in the workforce and leading a full like generally.

Death and dying Phobia: Thanatophobia, the fear of dying, a death anxiety is a "feeling of dread, apprehension or solicitude when one thinks of the process of dying, or ceasing to 'be'" . Necrophobia is a specific phobia which is the irrational fear of dead things (e.g., corpses) as well as things associated with death (e.g., coffins, tombstones, funerals, cemeteries).

Relationship Anxiety: Otherwise know as Jealousy happens most commonly within a romantic relationship, although it can occur between siblings and other family members, in friendships and in professional relationships. A small amount of anxiety/Jealousy can be good. For example, if it's mild and well managed it can help a couple to appreciate each other and add to the passion of a relationship. But extreme anxiety/Jealousy can destroy relationships and damage your health. When someone feels jealous, they feel that someone or a situation is threatening something that they value highly, especially a relationship. Jealousy can make you feel angry, anxious and threatened. You might become hyper vigilant, oversensitive and possessive

Generalised Anxiety Disorder: Excessive worry about some areas of life and it leads to a sense of demoralisation. The cycle is started by the type of thinking psychotherapists call 'the what if' this then leads to a spiraling in mood as the worries become uncontrollable which then leads to a demoralised state. Also if you have 3 or more of the above types of anxiety then doctors will diagnose you as having one diagnosis of GAD.

Uncovering Common Causes of Anxiety

Many people believe that anxiety "just happens," but this is never true. It is preceded by avoidance of one's usual activities and a flagging of interest in daily goings-on that then leads to thoughts of loss. Moving from an unconscious process to a conscious one with the sudden dawning of the reality of their lives. People tend to damn themselves because they feel stuck; some eventually find a way out, but others don't get out and continue to feel stuck, which in turn leads to actual anxiety. Here are some of the most common reasons people begin to experience anxiety:

- Problems like shyness, social anxiety, worry, and obsessional symptoms can be passed down through generations
- Communication problems that stem from unhelpful anger may cause others to look away, causing you to avoid interacting with them in turn.
- Constant worry about what others think of you can lead to attention deficits.
- You attribute good reasons for excessive worry like "If I worry it shows I care and If I don't worry then it shows I don't care".

- Experiencing racism, homophobia, or sexism, particularly for those unable to stand up and assert themselves.
- Passive behaviour, such as staying in the same unrewarding job for years.
- Geneticism, as when an adopted person is not treated equally to the adoptive parents' biological children.

These reasons often lead to choices being made that initially help us seem to escape or to protect ourselves; these may initially result in feeling better but over time can lead to isolation and withdrawal from society. It's important to recognise that the mind is both your friend and your enemy. It appears to give friendly advice—for instance, stay away from that pain or stay with certain people—but, in fact, it is advice that can lead you down a path of avoidance.

Pit Stop Exercise: Take a moment now to identify one instance each of something you believed to be friendly advice and enemy advice coming from your mind that eventually led to avoidance. This will help you to identify thoughts, actions, emotions, choices, or relationships that ultimately proved to be self-destructive. It's good to break down anxiety in this way, as it provides you with some ideas to reflect upon. We will come back to the idea of self-reflection again later.

Identifying What Fuels Anxiety
Fig 1.1 A basic model to show how anxiety is fuelled

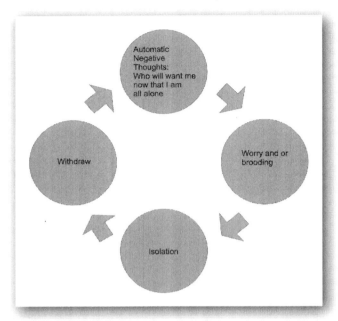

Isolation leads you to withdraw from friends and family, and to not live up to your overall ideas about how your life should proceed, This tends to lead to feeling stuck, to feeling as though your life is not moving forward.

Let's take a look at one example of what I call an Idea for Living (IFL):
Idea for Living: Fatherhood

I want to be a father who is warm, approachable, and consistent. I want to extend a caring hand to my children to ensure they know they are loved and learn right from wrong.

If you are anxious, you probably realise that being stuck in bed and brooding about the coulda-shoulda-wouldas is moving you away from that IFL—but you may feel powerless to change your situation regardless.

What steps can you take to move towards the IFL for fatherhood? It may be that you can think of only one action: go with it. One simple action may have a domino effect, resulting in other actions that then lead to lifting your overall mood. Like for instance instead of ignoring your child's request for bedtime reading to act against the feeling and go rather to the idea for living. By reading one story it may lead to another positive behaviour like giving your child a good night kiss. But what happens to the Automatic Negative Thoughts (ANTs)? Allow them to exist in your mind, like a balloon floating on a string. You may be tempted to want to pop the balloon, but if you can acknowledge its presence without letting it distract you while you commit to a new action, gradually other thoughts will come: Automatic Realistic Thoughts (ARTs).

Fig 1.2 Table on Idea for Living

Ideas for Living chart

Intimacy- Do you want to be a warm, giving, authentic, genuine, forgiving, caring, trustworthy, self accepting person	Spirituality-Are you involved in organized religion or just spiritual spending moments by yourself? If so have you let this lapse and need to discover again your spirituality?
Social-Do you want to be community focused, volunteering, providing parties, life and soul of party, thoughtful, caring person	Politics-Do you believe passionately but now don't bother? Are you a libertarian, Tory, Liberal, or labour voter?
Mental Health-Do you want to be proud of being a person who shares about how they feel, their thoughts, actions and that being vulnerable is a sign of strength and good mental health	Parenthood-Do you want to be caring, shy, outrageous, cool, pedantic, easy going, generous, cautious, colourful, intelligent, creative, stern, disciplinarian etc
Leisure-Do you want to be active in sports, reading, swimming, cooking, interpretation, art, movie watching, debating, riding, cycling, rambling etc	Work-What type of worker do you want to be? Warm, easy going, strict, earnest, patient, kind, log suffering, energetic, autonomous, allowing delegation, permitting attitude etc
Sexuality-Are you wanting to be the best gay, lesbian, bisexual, transgendered, transvestite, curious person who likes to define their sexuality by different ways rather than living to other expectations?	Ethnicity/Culture-Do you hide away from the person you were born to be? Instead is it time to be proud and find ways from your ethnicity/Culture that can help relax you and bring energy into your life.
Gender-What kind of man or woman do you want to be? Is it a strong minded, intellectual, fun, bubbly, serious, thoughtful, energetic, passive, peaceful etc	Genetic- (This is about those who have been adopted. Do you want to lead a life that your parents have helped create for you or do you want to capture something from your birth parents? Do you want to be remembered as being from a certain back ground, ethnicity, Culture, country

Fig 1.3 TRAP of Anxiety

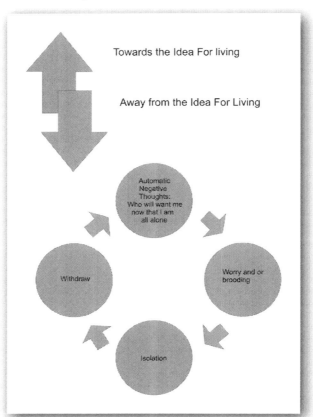

A Brief Look at the Emotions That Occur Alongside Anxiety

Many emotions fill up those boxes in the anxiety warehouse. It can be difficult to know how to deal with overwhelming emotions. "Emotional intelligence" is a term you may have heard used by psychotherapists—it refers to being able to acknowledge your emotions and to have the capacity for being self-aware. Let's look at some common feelings, many of which fall under the umbrella of one of seven underlying emotions:

- *Anxiety*: vexed, worried, agitated, apprehensive, edgy, crabby, concerned, fearful, scared, troublesome, jumpy, nervous
- *Anger*: annoyed, irritated, bad-tempered, aggressive, cross, unpleasant, furious, hostile, touchy, livid
- *Shame*: humiliated, mortified, dishonored, disgraced, disrespected
- *Jealousy*: suspicious, wary, paranoid, anxious
- *Hurt*: gutted, offended, rejected, brokenhearted, aggrieved, downhearted
- *Guilt*: blameworthy, at fault, sinful, unforgivable, deserving of punishment, answerable
- *Joy*: euphoric, ecstatic, aware of beauty, grateful
- *Depressed*: feeling lost, punished, unwanted, down, overwhelmed.

———————

Pit Stop Exercise: Spend five minutes now on learning how to notice and describe your feelings. Close your eyes. Focus on your breathing. Describe what you notice, which may just be how your chest rises and falls with each breath. Then, focus on how you are seated and on the imprint your body is making in the chair. The key here is to notice and describe without making a judgment: "I notice that my hands are resting in my lap, my legs are together, and both feet are flat on the floor." Next, move your attention to sounds within the room and describe what you notice. Repeat this process just as impartially with your thoughts and feelings. Remember: just because you think or feel something does not mean you have to act on it. Just stay in the chair, observing your present experience with sounds, thoughts, and emotions. This five-minute exercise can be useful in changing your relationship with your own emotions and intrusive thoughts.

———————

Table 1.1 Helpful and unhelpful negative emotions.

Emotion	Helpful or unhelpful	Inference in personal domain	Type of belief	Cognitive consequence	Urge/action/behaviour
Anxiety	Unhelpful	Threat or danger	unhelpful	You overestimate the negative features of the threat / You underestimate your ability to cope with the threat / You create an even more negative threat in your mind / You have more task-irrelevant thoughts than when you're concerned	To withdraw physically from the threat / To withdraw mentally from the threat / To ward off the threat (for example, by superstitious behaviour) / To tranquilise feelings / To seek reassurance
Concern	Helpful	Threat or danger	Helpful	You view the threat realistically / You realistically appraise your ability to cope with the threat / You don't create an even more negative threat in your mind / You have more task-relevant thoughts than when you're anxious	To face up to the threat / To deal with the threat constructively
Depression	Unhelpful	Loss (with implications for the future) / Failure	Unhelpful	You see only negative aspects of the loss or failure / You think of other losses and failures that you've experienced / You think you're unable to help yourself (helplessness) / You only see pain and blackness in the future (hopelessness)	To withdraw from reinforcements / To withdraw into yourself / To create an environment consistent with feelings / To attempt to put a stop to feelings of depression in self-destructive ways
Sadness	Helpful	Loss (with implications for the future) / Failure	Helpful	You're able to see both negative and positive aspects of your loss or failure / You're less likely to think of other losses and failures than when you're depressed / You're able to help yourself / You're able to look to the future with hope	To express feelings about the loss or failure and talk about these to significant others / To seek out reinforcements after a period of mourning

Unhelpful anger	Unhelpful	Frustration Self or other transgress personal rule Threat to self esteem	You overestimate the extent to which the other person acted deliberately You see malicious intent in the motives of other people You see yourself as definitely right and other(s) as definitely wrong You're unable to see the other person's point of view You plot to exact revenge	To attack the other person physically To attack the other person verbally To attack the other person passive-aggressively To displace the attack onto another person, animal, or object To withdraw aggressively To recruit allies against the other person
Annoyance	Helpful	Frustration Self or other transgress personal rule Threat to self esteem	You don't overestimate the extent to which the other person acted deliberately You don't see malicious intent in the motives of the other(s) You don't see yourself as definitely right or other(s) as definitely wrong You're able to see the other(s) point of view You don't plot to exact revenge	To assert yourself with the other person To request, but not demand behavioural change from the other person
Guilt	Unhelpful	Violation of your moral code (sin of commission) Failure to live up to your moral code (sin of omission) You hurt the feelings of a significant other	You assume you have definitely committed the sin You assume more personal responsibilities than the situation warrants You assign far less responsibility to other people than is warranted You don't think of mitigating factors You don't put your behaviour into its overall context You expect to receive retribution	To escape from the unhealthy pain of guilt in self-defeating ways To beg forgiveness from the person wronged To promise unrealistically that she won't 'sin' again To punish yourself physically or by deprivation (self harm) To disclaim responsibility for wrongdoing
Remorse	Helpful	Violation of your moral code (sin of commission) Failure to live up to your moral code (sin of omission) You hurt the feelings of a	You consider behaviours in context and with understanding in making a final judgement about whether you've 'sinned' You assume an appropriate level of personal responsibility You assign an appropriate level of responsibility to other people	To face up to the healthy pain that accompanies the realisation that you've sinned To ask, but not beg, for forgiveness To understand reasons for wrongdoing and to act on your understanding

		Situation	Inferences	Behaviours
Shame		... significant other	You take into account mitigating factors / You put behaviour into its overall context / You don't expect to receive retribution	To atone for the sin by taking a penalty / To make appropriate amends / No tendency to make excuses for your behaviour or enact other defensive behaviour
	Unhelpful	Something shameful has been revealed about self (or group with whom one identifies) by self or others / Other people look down upon or shun you (or the group with whom you identify)	You overestimate the 'shamefulness' of the information revealed / You overestimate the likelihood that the judging group will notice or be interested in the information / You overestimate the degree of disapproval (of reference group) you'll receive / You overestimate the length of time any disapproval will last	To remove yourself from the 'gaze' of others / To isolate yourself from others / To save face by attacking other(s) who have 'shammed' you / To defend threatened self-esteem in self-defeating ways / To ignore attempts by other people to restore social equilibrium
Disappointment	Helpful	Something shameful has been revealed about you (or the group with whom you identify) by yourself or other people / Other people look down upon or shun you (or the group with whom you identify)	You see information revealed in a compassionate self-accepting context / You're realistic about the likelihood that the judging group will notice or be interested in the information / You're realistic about the degree of disapproval (or reference group) you'll receive / You're realistic about the length of time any disapproval will last	To continue to participate actively in social interaction / To respond to attempts of other people to restore social stability
Hurt	Unhelpful	Other people treat you badly (self undeserving)	You overestimate the unfairness of the other person's behaviour / You perceive the other person as showing a lack of care or of being indifferent / You see yourself as alone, uncared for, or misunderstood / You tend to think of past 'hurts' / You thinks that the other person has to put things right of their own accord first	To shut down communication channels with the other person / To criticise the other person without disclosing what you feel hurt about
Sorrow	Helpful	Other people treat you badly	You're realistic about the degree of unfairness in the other person's	To communicate your feelings to the other

		(self undeserving)	behaviour	persondirectly
			You perceive the other(s) as acting badly rather than as uncaring or indifferent	To influence the other person to act in a fairer manner
			You don't see yourself as alone, uncared for, or misunderstood	
			You're less likely to think of past hurts than when hurt	
			You don't think that the other person has to make the first move	
Unhelpful jealousy	Unhelpful	Threat to your relationship with your partner from another person	You tend to see threats to your relationship when none really exists	To seek constant reassurance that you're loved
			You think the loss of your relationship is imminent	To monitor the actions and feelings of your partner
			You misconstrue your partner's ordinary conversations as having romantic or sexual connotations	To search for evidence that your partner is involved with someone else
			You construct visual images of your partner's infidelity	To attempt to restrict the movements or activities of your partner
			If your partner admits to finding another person attractive, you believe that he or she sees the other person as more attractive than yourself and that your partner will leave yourself for this other person	To set tests which your partner has to pass
				To retaliate for your partner's presumed infidelity
				To sulk
Helpful Jealousy	Helpful	Threat to your relationship with your partner from another person	You tend not to see threats to one's relationship when none exists	To allow your partner to express love without seeking reassurance
			You don't misconstrue your partner's ordinary conversations between your partner and other people	To allow your partner freedom without monitoring his/her feelings, actions, and whereabouts
			You don't construct visual images of infidelity	To allow your partner to show natural interest in members of the opposite sex without setting tests
			You accept that your partner finds other people attractive but don't see this as a threat	
Unhelpful envy	Unhelpful	Another person possesses and enjoys something desirable that you don't have	You tend to denigrate the value of the desired possession and/or the person who possesses it	To disparage verbally the person who has the possession you desire
			You try to convince yourself that you're happy with your own	To disparage verbally the possession you

				desire
		possessions (although you're not)		To take away the possession you desire from the other person (either so that you have it or that you deprive the other person of it)
		You think about how to acquire the desired possession, regardless of its usefulness		To spoil or destroy the possession so that the other person does not have it
		You think about how to deprive the other person of the possession you desire		
		You honestly admit to yourself that you desire the possession		To strive to obtain the desired possession if it is truly what you want
Helpful envy	Helpful	Another person possesses and enjoys something desirable that you don't have	You don't try to convince yourself that you're happy with your own possession when you're not	
			You think about how to obtain the desired possession because you desires it for healthy reasons	
		Helpful	You can allow the person to have and enjoy the desired possession without denigrating the person or the possession	

16

Emotional Responsibility

Once you become aware of your emotions and how they affect you, you will be in a better position to acknowledge how they alter your behavior and move forward. Thinking your way through your feelings requires focusing on a goal for how you would *like* to behave whenever you experience a certain feeling. When you imagine that feeling now, can you be honest with yourself about how you are likely to react? Does this differ from acting in line with the behaviour you want to exhibit? This is what psychotherapists call Behaviour Activation—the process of activating a new behaviour despite not having the motivation to do so.

The wait between acknowledging that you would *like* to act differently in a given situation and *being* able to act differently can be a very long one. I like to use the analogy of delayed luggage at the airport: luggage sometimes gets lost during a journey, but *eventually* you receive it. It's OK to acknowledge that you don't feel like acting in the way you know you would like to, but try to encourage yourself to just do it! Experiment with this. Rate your mood before and after an instance where you either allowed yourself to act in the old, ingrained way and after an instance where you compelled yourself to act in the new way. Is there a marked difference? I guarantee that you will see your mood improving just for having analysed your own behaviour.

In the next chapter, we will go into more detail about changing behaviour.

If you want to feel differently, you have to start by actively changing the way you think and behave. There can be no emotional change without a corresponding change in your behaviour.

Behaviour Activation Form example. 0 = low in mood and 10 = bright in mood. With chores, for example, you might feel a sense of achievement. Rate 0 = no feeling of achievement and 10 = high feeling of achievement.

Fig 1.4 Mood chart

	Rate mood before activity	Pleasure activity	Rate mood after activity	Rate mood before chore activity	Chore Activity	Rate mood after activity
Sunday	0/10	Going to feed the ducks	7/10	0/10	Washing the dog	7/10
Monday						

Fig 1.4 Mood chart

Making Sense of the Symptoms

Two useful ways of viewing anxiety is of the bully or overfed dog. A bully waits for you in the corridor to take your lunch money and to tell you what you can and cannot do. Do you stand up to the bully and tell him to push off? If you cannot image yourself doing that then imagine the anxiety as an overfed dog and you need to reduce the feeds by two daily from thirty times daily; working your way down to the dog becoming fit again and receiving two feeds daily. If you have tried this with an over-weigh dog you will know hoe difficult it is as the dog will pester you for the two missing feeds but eventually you reach the middle way and the attention of the dog is upon the recent missing feeds not the ones form the beginning of the process. Anxiety is like an overfed dog and when you reduce the self defeating behaviours like for example reassurance seeking then the anxiety will pester you for the missing behaviours and you have to stay strong and firm to your goals. Anxiety does not have to hold you back. You can learn to weave it into the tapestry of your life—and still come away with a great work of art. When you are low in mood, ask yourself: Is this me or the bully or the overfed dog talking? If it's the bully or the overfed dog, then do encourage yourself to take the appropriate emotion action.

Example: A man who is adopted by Mr. and Mrs. Smith realises that he has been treated differently from his brother and sisters, who are their biological children. When he learns that the birth siblings are receiving more financial help, he feels anxious. He is tempted to isolate himself from them all, to withdraw from the family meetings. The more he isolates himself, though, the more easily sadness edges towards depression. He broods on the injustice of his predicament.

The bully will lead him to further despair. He will question the value of his role within the family, fixate on the life he might have had with his own birth family, and on how his partner perceives his history. If allowed, the bully will cause havoc—doing whatever he wants and destroying everything around him.

What could the man do instead? He will have to voluntarily wrestle with difficult questions about his identity and being adopted, and this is likely to take a long time. But rather than isolate himself, he could go for a "checking in" behaviour instead. The bully wants him to isolate and brood, but the apposite emotion action would be to check in with the adoptive parents and let them know he finds their behaviour hurtful. This gives them the opportunity to discuss the situation and possibly remedy it. Helpful negative emotions can lead to connecting with others and being able to gather new information, whereas unhelpful negative emotions lead only to withdrawal.

Appetite Changes

Overeating and undereating are very common behaviours for people who are attempting to fill a void of some sort. Sugary foods, which are often sought out by those with a tendency to overeat, can give a short-term kick but they ultimately lead to long term burn out since they contain little of nutritional value. Undereaters often claim not to "be in the mood" to eat, which is a thinking pattern indicative of depression which sometimes can come alongside anxiety. This is called Emotional Reasoning, and may lead to refusing to eat or not enjoying food in general.

Its important to keep in mind that food is an investment that will help your body provide good returns. Vitamin B in the diet, for example, helps the absorption of other minerals and nutrients needed for thinking, energy, good sleep, good sex, and general well-being. Iron is essential for transporting oxygen in the blood cells. Protein helps with thinking, alertness, and general productivity in the day.

———

Pit Stop Exercise: Carry out a food monitoring diary and record what you eat and drink in the week. You will be surprised how just looking at the diary at the end of the week can help you tweak it to add or subtract items when it comes to week 2.

———

Feelings of Being Punished and Other Common Thoughts
When Albert Ellis and Aaron Beck, the grandfathers of cognitive psycho-therapies, started on their quest to establish Rational Emotive Behaviour Therapy and Cognitive Therapy, they both discovered one experience that was common among many people suffering from anxiety: a feeling of being overwhelmed seeing things in a catastrophic manner. Beck went on to create a questionnaire called the Beck Anxiety Inventory, which assesses symptoms commonly experienced by sufferers of anxiety. Ellis went on to develop a list of twelve common irrational beliefs/attitudes that underpin anxiety:

- I must be successful at all times; if I am not, then life is awful and I can't tolerate it
- I must get approval from all people at all times
- I must be loved by significant people at all times
- I have acted badly and deserve to be punished
- I must be competent, adequate, or high-achieving in all important aspects of my life; if I am not, then I am worthless
- It is awful when things don't go my way
- My emotional upset is caused by others; I have no control over how they make me feel
- I cannot face life's difficulties, nor should I have to
- There is a solution for everything; the fact that I cannot find one is awful and terrible

- ◆ I must be dependent on others; I need them
- ◆ Others must act with consideration and with fairness; they are terrible villains if they do not
- ◆ I cannot stop thinking about bad things over and over

Let's Take a Step Back and See If the Life You Have Now Has Shrunk

Anxiety causes people to reduce activity levels, cancel engagements, eat differently, and sleep differently. A process of "de-conditioning" also often takes place, which leads to the idea that you deserve to be being punished. De-conditioning is a term psychotherapists use to describe a process of breaking your daily structure for one that has no structure and for allowing yourself to be led by how you feel rather than by what you know is good for you. In my experience, anxiety patients advised to get busy rather than to sleep and rest often do better. The "bully" needs to know who is the leader—YOU! Try to shut out the mind when it says you deserve to be punished; realise that this is the bully talking and do something different. Take hold of the bully and tell him to push off.

Filling the Void with Junk

When we are anxious, we often describe feelings of boredom, needing to seek others' approval, and not being comfortable in our own skin. We tend to fill the void that anxiety—and its associated reduction of activity levels—leaves behind with other things like approval-seeking, drinking to block out boredom, and self-defeating habits to avoid feeling uncomfortable feelings. Think of trying instead to be like a bed-and-breakfast owner: open your door to any visitor and welcome them with coffee and biscuits. Sit and chat with them. If your tendency is to avoid others, make yourself aware of when you're having uncomfortable thoughts and feelings, then focus your attention on breathing into them. Gradually, with each practice, you will be better able to deal head-on with the thought or feeling, and finding your own healthy way of coping with it.

Try also:

+ A good night's sleep
+ Healthy diet
+ Meaningful activity
+ Mental stimulation
+ Mentalisation
+ Work-life balance
+ Enjoy life by doing a little bit of what you fancy

Tip: Being able to sit still without being actively entertained—that is, being bored—is an important skill to pass on to your children. Being able to amuse oneself using ordinary pastimes like reading, writing, or simply watching people through a window or at café is a liberating gift to pass on to the next generation.

Psychobabble defined: Mentalisation is the skill of understanding other people's intentions according to present relationships rather than past ones. Mentalisation relates to how people make sense of their social world by imagining how other peoples' states of mind that could influence their behaviour. It offers doubt as a viable option for dealing with distress

Inability to Concentrate

Anxiety results in high levels of cortisol being produced; in turn, this "stress hormone" causes the brain's problem-solving area to work less efficiently. This leads to feelings of inadequacy because of a lack of ability to concentrate; the more stressed you become, the less effective you feel. This downward spiral can quickly turn into a catastrophe. Attitudes that are useful for combating this are such as: "It's OK," "It's not the end of the world," and "I will try again later." It's important to give yourself a Pause button and to tell yourself that you can always try again later. Take small steps. Remember: tackling anxiety is like a dance where you will take two steps forward and one step back. Eventually, you will get across the dance floor and be a great moving daddy dancer!

Irritability

It's natural for all of us to feel irritable at some point; in people suffering from anxiety, it's a sure sign of unhelpful stress. When you are unable to concentrate, irritability sets in alongside restlessness, a lack of sleep, and feeling stuck. Sometimes this irritation can even disrupt relationships because it can easily lead to angry outbursts. Energy levels in people suffering from anxiety are already down, but the less you attempt to do, the worse it will be. The key here is to reengage with family, friends, and work to keep the channels of communication open and flowing freely. Be kind and forgiving to yourself. Allow for compassion to grow within by helping out family, by donating your time, or by giving your talents as a gift to others—it can be as simple as baking a cake or making a birthday card for a relative or friend.

Lacking Pleasure and Enjoyment in Things

In anxiety, the brain goes into a rationing mode where it only allows the most important functions to operate. To conserve energy, it will "want" to cut out more high-maintenance items like socializing, meeting family, enjoying hobbies, etc. It will focus on more low-maintenance options like sleeping, brooding, etc.—behaviours that lead to isolation. The brain is trying to conserve energy and to protect itself, but in fact it's making things worse and you feel depressed.

———

Pit Stop Exercise: On a piece of paper, draw a weeklong calendar. Write down what activities you did in the last week. Include wake-up times, mealtimes, watching TV, bedtimes, sex, etc. When you have finished, go through each one and rate your mood during that activity. Let zero equal a low mood and ten equal a bright mood. Go through each activity again, noting which improved your mood and which lowered your mood or made it worse.

———

Low Mood

It can be soul-destroying to experience an immediate punch of low mood the first thing in the morning. This pattern can be difficult to change and can plague you day after day. The task here is to get to know yourself—are you willing to take the challenge to do this? For instance, life today is fast-paced and the everyday pleasures of the past are being phased out for modernity. Wood fires, for example, are a simple pleasure and one that bring calm and tranquillity. Try to think about other simple things you like but have not done or experienced for a while and get to know yourself by writing in your positive data log. By keeping a log will help the mind to remember positives more easily thus remedy low moods first thing in the morning

Seeking Isolation from Other People

With anxiety, the mind often pretends to be your friend when in fact it's acting as your enemy. If you believe your mind is your friend always, then you are going to suffer a lot; if you see that, at times it will be your friend and at other times it will be the enemy, then you will be able to *respond* to situations rather than just to *react* to them. This helps you to be more aware of your choices. One of the key ways the mind acts as an unhelpful influence in depression is by suggesting to us that we avoid our friends, family, and colleagues.

———

Pit Stop Exercise: Look at your calendar for the last week. Which activities would you add again to this week's calendar? Try to add the ones that you know improve your mood. Then add activities that you used to enjoy but haven't participated in lately. Last, include some that take you out of your comfort zone. Be daring!! Don't forget to rate your mood before and after each activity as they happen. This schedule is like drawing up a contract with yourself. If you don't feel like doing it, consider yourself contractually obliged to just do it anyway. You'll be glad you did!

———

Self-Harm

Is anything that you do harmful to you? Look beyond the obvious and most violent activities like cutting, overdosing, boozing, and doing drugs. For instance: starting arguments, bickering, and sulking can be constant sources of distress and maybe part of a dynamic in a relationship that is harmful. Remember that you need to consider your relationship with yourself, and ask yourself what actions may be harmful to that If you find some, then you need to ask yourself how badly you want it to change. Many who self-harm view it as a way to self-soothe in response to difficult thoughts, feelings, actions, and memories. This may be the only defense mechanism you have now, but there are many other ways to self-soothe; these may feel alien to you initially, but will help the more you develop the skills involved.

———

Pit Stop Exercise: When you feel the urge to self-harm but you are consciously trying not to carry out self-defeating behaviours, simply go to the bathroom and treat yourself to a bath or shower. As you draw the water, feel it pass through your fingers. Concentrate on the sensations of the water on your hands, add some bubble bath solution, and smell the fragrance of the soaps. Look around you at the steam fogging up the mirrors. Get undressed at a slower pace than usual and take time to feel the ritual of the movements. Step into the water and wash your body slowly. This is a skill to be practiced over and over; it can help you to place any harmful urges on hold. Consider doing something nice for yourself as a reward for getting to that step.

———

Sex Drive

Anxious people often experience a reduced sex drive. This is due in part to the reduction of a neurotransmitter in the brain called serotonin. Its job is to help us feel happy, excited, and to give us increased energy to do things. In chronic cases of anxiety another problem of depression may follow; in depression there is a reduction in serotonin levels; the imbalance will continue until you receive therapy and/or medication designed to increase serotonin production, which creates better moods and an overall feeling of happiness. This group of antidepressant medications is called Selective Serotonin Reuptake Inhibitors, or SSRIs. Some of these drugs are effective for anxiety too

A reduction in serotonin leads to low interest in sex; you may therefore decline your partner's advances and potentially do harm to your relationship. Exercise, however, increases the number of endorphins in your bloodstream, which also can improve mood. Try viewing sex as exercise and see how adventurous you can be together with your partner. Remember: the biggest sex organ is the BRAIN! Use it to stimulate yourself and your partner. There is more to sex than just penetration—there is massage, talking about fantasies, talking about how much you love the other person and what you find sexy about him or her, writing down your fantasies, spanking, dressing up, and incorporating food, ice cubes, candles, etc. Give it a go.

Thoughts of Suicide

Many anxiety sufferers unfortunately cannot shake the idea that they are alone in feeling as they do. Some experience thoughts of suicide for reasons like hating themselves so much that they want to punish themselves; at its most basic, this is a problem-solving issue where the sufferer will think it would best to end his or her life for the sake of the family. Honor is a huge issue for many families, who find mental illness shameful, weak, or intolerable—this often has cultural roots. Considerations of "honor" need to be thrown out with the garbage, as they have no place in your recovery.

Cultures can send people complicated messages; the influence of societal pressures has been discussed in academic circles for decades, but it can be used to promote an ideology or to belittle another person for the sake of the majority and or a group's history. But culture lives—now more than ever it's defined as what the ordinary people living today decide it should be, not what dead people decided it should be centuries ago. Culture ought to be a protective, evolving influence that helps people lead the best lives they can.

Culture plays an even more involved role for the LGBT community. Many men and women sadly commit suicide because they are not allowed to live openly as a gay person. In fact, 60 percent of British citizens from Pakistani origins are forced into marriage abroad; every fifty-two minutes, police are called to respond to a woman in distress due to domestic violence; a woman is murdered every two weeks in the UK. The issue of family honor and culture needs to be fully addressed in another book— don't suffer in silence, though, there are support groups out there for every persuasion.

Fact Corner: Many people believe that if someone is having thoughts of suicide then a person might act without thinking and do it. This is not true; it is simply a sign that the illness is getting worse and the anxious person needs help. Contact a GP, nurse or psychotherapist immediately. Talking therapies can help you get out from under anxiety and start feeling good again.

Starting Out on Your Journey into Mindfulness

Mindfulness-Based Cognitive Therapy (MBCT) has its roots in the Buddhist practice of meditation. Scientists studied certain aspects of that centuries-old tradition and developed it into what we know as MBCT today. It focuses on incorporating the aspects of meditation that have a positive effect on the brain, but does not contain any religious element. Staggering results have shown that distress centres in the brain are significantly reduced during meditation, bringing about relief. Science has now proven what Buddhists have known for over two thousand years—it's effective. Research is still ongoing, and the psychotherapy world continues to share results.

Introducing the Basic Principles of Mindfulness

Mindfulness is about learning to develop an awareness of yourself and your surroundings. Learning to understand the mental events that we call thoughts, urges, actions, images, feelings, and sensations. Learning how the mind processes and copes with these events. What kind of events make the mind try to block things out, freeze, or pull back? We have developed techniques to help you look at your own mind by taking a step back from your own emotions, and registering them as an observer. This process always leads to some interesting discoveries.

Walking the Path of Self-Discovery

To learn the most about yourself, treat your everyday experiences with curiosity—as if you have never done them before. Try walking to work as if for the first time and make a mental note of what you see that you never noticed on any other day. Self-discovery is often as simple as slowing down. You will learn much by detaching yourself for a moment from this stressed-out world and watching it as an outsider, then describing what you notice.

Thriving by Doing Less and Noticing More

If passersby looked in through the window of my clinic, they would see a bunch of people with their eyes closed, seemingly doing nothing. Really, of course, they are doing a lot to rebuild and repair themselves mentally and emotionally. They are learning to slow down and watch the frantic race of life from the detached perspective of their mind's eye. Doing less is extremely difficult at first, but when achieved, it can help tremendously with anxiety; it can also help you stay well longer and help give you a perspective that is energetic, exhilarating, calm, passionate, reflective, and peaceful.

Moving from Anxiety towards Mindful Well-Being

Anxiety is on a mission to shut things down slowly. It sends messages to your body to conserve energy, so the brain will tell you to take a nap, sleep more, eat less, socially exclude yourself from social situations—all ostensibly with the aim of self-preservation. But this is NOT helping you! Instead, the more you reduce your activity level, the worse your anxiety will get. Anxiety also creates two types of circular thinking: brooding and worrying. Brooding is the "coulda, should, woulda" type of thinking about the past, and worry is the "What if? What if?" The latter makes you feel as though you're always thinking about minute details and is concerned with the future. The ability to think in the present is severely reduced by both, so we'll start in the here and now first.

———

Pit Stop Exercise: Look around and describe an object somewhere near you now, but without judgment. Do it again with another object, describing only what you notice. Then try—with your eyes closed—to describe a mental event like a thought, urge, image, feeling etc. that you notice you are having.

———

For example, as I write this I notice the sensations of a tightening of the chest, the rushing of the blood, and a tingling feeling in the hands. Anxiety is passing through me, and my thoughts are darting around from one topic to another rapidly; my mind is trying to catch them to block them out. I take a mental "step back" to watch the sequence of happenings as they occur, without trying to stop them.

By stepping back and simply remarking what you feel; a lot of information can be gained. Remember to try this exercise in a seated position. You do not have to react to the thoughts, but instead just notice them and describe them without judgment. I did not place a judgment on my experience like "I cannot stand it when I can't seem to focus."

CHAPTER 2

Challenging Your Anxiety

In This Chapter You Will

- ◆ Get to the crux of your anxiety and learn tools to help you
- ◆ Look at Ideas for Living to gain a bigger perspective
- ◆ Start your journey with Mindfulness-Based Cognitive Therapy

Once you get to know your individual cycle of anxiety and how you adapt to it, the next step is to get to the crux of it and challenge it. This is easier said than done, but with some key ideas it can be achieved. In this chapter, I will introduce to you the first phase of mindfulness: developing tools to tackle some of the main problems in depression such as an inability to concentrate and difficulties with problem solving. By using the ideas here, your confidence will grow because you will feel that you are getting back to your old self again—or maybe your old self but with a twist of something different!

Entering the Beginner Mind

Our minds are fraught with preoccupations, and they bounce from one thing to the next. Technology has become a big part of modern life, and with it comes multitasking that exceeds anything like what generations before were expected to accomplish. The mind is capable of so much, but to ignore certain of its rules is to put yourself in peril. The key to developing yourself is the rule of awareness, which will help you to enjoy the path to the wise mind—more on that later. In your first practices with mindfulness meditation, the mind will move away from you a thousand times; it's your job to bring your awareness back to the present moment every time. The mind will not yet have the discipline to focus, so the first phase of MBCT is about bringing discipline to the mind.

———

Pit Stop Exercise: Close your eyes if you wish. Focus your attention on the movement of your belly as you breathe in and out. Keep your back straight if seated or supported if lying down. Try to practice this without distraction for three minutes.

———

Wake Up! Realising That You're on Autopilot

You likely take the same car journey again and again—say to the market and back every weekend. But what do you notice along the way? Chances are that you don't have a clue. Because the route is familiar to you, you essentially go on autopilot. Similarly, the mind will take for granted repeat information and just carry out routine actions without analysing anything about them. To truly think is to slow things down. The brain does not want to do that. The brain processes information very quickly in order to be efficient. The downside of this processing power is that we forget to see the ordinary, everyday beauty around us, and how it can bring joy to our otherwise fast-paced life.

Switching On Your Problem-Solving Ability

Unhealthy stress switches off the problem-solving centre in the brain. This leads to a mood that spirals lower and lower, which in turn leads to depression. Constant self-criticism that occurs when we feel defeated, and we feel defeated when we are unable to solve problems efficiently or easily. This is just how we are wired. If you find yourself struggling at any given moment, take it as a signal that you need to help yourself. Daily meditation is a perfect way to create "time in" for yourself and to start developing a relationship with yourself. This brings about relaxation and a calmness of the mind, which can switch the problem-solving ability "on" again, thus helping you to start feeling some normality.

Getting Your Concentration Level Back on Track

It is normal for concentration to be considerably reduced when anxious, but doing what psychotherapists call Attention-Training Exercises can build your mental stamina up again. By using sounds, we can focus on them and then move our attention to other sounds. By moving attention from one sound to another, we can improve concentration. This is discussed more fully in Chapter 3.

Accepting That Too Much Control Is Bad for You

Are you a control freak? Often, trying too hard to get or stay in control is energy draining and self-defeating. In fact, some of our most important life events give us little or no control over them. You did not get to choose your parents, neither did you have control over where you were born or over which social class you were born into. Rather than adopting a demanding attitude and trying to control everything, try to consider alternatives. Could it be liberating to think that I had no control over where I was educated, qualified, or even whom I wound up married to because my value system comes from my parents and this largely has influenced my life, for example?

You could have been born to drug lords in another country; that life would likely be very different to the one you have now. The control you *do* have is over the present moment. You can choose to connect with the person with you right now, or not. If you connect, then you develop authenticity with that person, and you might surprise yourself at how much you enjoy the process. I say "surprise" because you are opening yourself to new possibilities! We don't have control over what happens an hour from now. Yes, we know that we need to catch the bus to work perhaps, but who knows what may happen? We are under the control of other influences, like bus company timetables, engine failure, a medical emergency, etc. We can't expend energy worrying about every possibility; we must learn to worry about dealing with unexpected occurrences only if and when they happen.

Reflecting on Your Ideas for Living

Anxiety has an ability to make you feel stuck and unable to move forward. We are wired to impose values or ideas for living on ourselves. They help us move forward and achieve. Take this one, for fatherhood: "I want to be the best father; one who is a stickler for the rules but who is also capable of enjoying spontaneous moments while developing a relationship with my beautiful son." To keep this thought at the forefront of his mind, that father developed what I call ACTIONS. These included reading at bedtime, attending sports days, homework supervision, playing games, teaching the son to bake, etc. My own Idea for Living pertaining to work is: I want to be the best therapist I can be because this brings excitement and purpose to my life. ACTIONS: meet new clients, assess their problems, treat their problems, connect with clients, value the connections I make, etc. Try writing some Ideas for Living (IFL) down, then consider how they affect each other. If I achieve my goals for work, it makes me feel good about myself, and in turn I will be a better father; my child benefits by receiving quality time.

Considering How You Would Like to Live or Be Remembered

Anxiety has this hold that is unshakable at first because you believe all the lies that anxiety tells you. Its time for a shake up and challenge yourself by asking two questions. One: How would I like to be remembered? Two: How would I like to think about myself? Or, if you want to be more emotive, then ask yourself: What would I like to have written on my epitaph? "Here lies a man who became defeated by the world and did not acknowledge his anxiety" or "Here lies a man who acknowledged he was suffering from anxiety and stood up to be counted"? Acknowledging that you have an issue is a sign of strength—it's shows you're at one with your vulnerabilities.

As a husband or wife? How do you want to be remembered as some-one's life partner? As one who was aggressive, or one who was attentive, caring, and a good listener? The choice is yours.

As a worker? Many of us get stuck in a rut and look at work only as a means of trying to extract as much money from an employer as possible. Instead, think what you could do for your boss or company to make them successful and prosperous! Or, if you are the boss, think about looking after your workers by doing something special for them. It's time to think outside the box and not to follow the status quo. Develop a difference that may stem from your cultural heritage, experiences, and life's work. Dare to inspire or dare to allow yourself to be inspired! Everyone remembers an inspired boss or colleague

As a parent? Parents tend to place too much pressure on themselves, especially at moments like the morning school run or when waiting at the school gates to collect the children. Be the parent you want to be; if that means breaking the mould, then do it. There are many different types of families now other than the traditional nuclear family. There are single parents, gay parents, small extended families where grandparents raise the children, large extended families where cousins or siblings raise children as well as the grandparents, etc. Research conducted in The Netherlands has shown that children with single parents and gay parents are on a par both emotionally and academically with children from nuclear families and in some cases are high achievers.

As a business owner? It's important to develop a business you are proud of, not just one built for the cold reason of simply earning money. Be the boss you were born to be and learn all you can about being a kind and good businessperson. How do you want to be thought of by your peers? Staff? Your family? If none of these are of interest to you, then consider how important your health is and follow your conscience. Normally, when you betray your own conscience, the effects manifest themselves in physical problems like lack of sleep or loss of appetite, stress, irritability, and avoidance. It's important to know yourself; your conscience is your barometer.

As an artist? Many produce only what they think others want from them. Approval-seeking behaviour is bad for us if done too much, and it can destroy creativity. Being true to yourself ought to be an Idea for Living that you seek, as this is the essence of yourself and one that is the cement for the other IFLs.

Fig 2.1 The Life-Shrinkage Model

Understanding the Life-Shrinkage Model

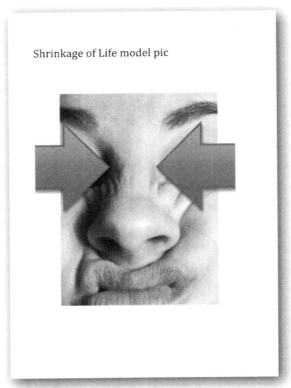

Shrinkage of Life model pic

This being the life that you once had is no longer the vibrant, loving life due to making wrong decisions or choices. The friends and family have gone and you have no one to turn to. Many people listen to their thoughts too much, especially when they feel hurt or angry because someone did something bad to them. Our mind's natural defence is to urge us to disengage by avoiding the people who caused the hurt in the first place. There are many reasons why we discontinue things, change our minds about someone, or make life-changing decisions that can be catastrophic or can lead to isolation and withdrawal. At the time when we make an individual decision, it might not appear to be problematic.

Taken collectively, many small decisions to isolate ourselves by degrees gather into one big hole that we can't escape. This hole is depression. When depressed people look back over their lives, they can often only see what they have lost. This creates a sense that a larger-than-life force is punishing them.

Commonly, anxiety plays a part in decisions that lead to a reduction in life activities. Social anxiety is a classic example—it leads to cutting out social engagements. Excessive worrying can lead to the dissolution of a marriage—perhaps you only want to deal with yourself because you think others cause your worry or obsessional thinking. Many depressed people are simply looking to lead what they feel is a well-controlled life, one where doubt and uncertainty are not allowed. Eventually, when you cut enough things out, nothing is left. This is a very common experience of depression: Where has my life gone? We tell ourselves "I am useless," "I have lost too much!" "I am being punished."

Reengaging and Nurturing the Idea That Life Goes On

After you acknowledge that you are suffering from anxiety, the next step is to take responsibility for it and for your treatment. Blaming others is not going to help you. If you believe that others should be the ones to change their behaviour, not you, that will only leave you in a state of powerlessness. The reality is that others will just carry on with life. Have the last laugh.

———

Pit Stop Exercise: Take time now to think about the important first step in treating your anxiety: taking responsibility for yourself and your illness. Is it time for a change of mood? Is it time to tackle horrible, destructive thoughts? Are some thoughts intrusive? Don't worry about how others view you as you are reading this book—make a decision to move forward today! You deserve a anxiety-free life.

———

Try these self-affirming statements to get you going:

- I can do anything—there is always time
- I can keep a schedule—I will just do it
- There's a lot I can do—I will be able to cope
- My task is challenging, but not overwhelming
- If I don't know how to do something, then I will ask for help
- I will do things even though I don't feel like it
- I can bear not knowing all the facts
- It's never too late
- I feel uncertain, but the answers will come

Phase Two

SECOND LEG OF THE JOURNEY: GETTING
TO THE CRUX OF YOUR ANXIETY

CHAPTER 3

Becoming More Mindful

In This Chapter You Will

- Know that all thoughts are OK—keep them coming!
- Learn to take your own thoughts less personally
- Learn that from vulnerability comes personality and creativity

Life is full of stresses, which can compound and cause a downward spiral that ultimately ends in anxiety and ultimately a sense of loss. In this chapter, I will be showing you how to slow down in this stressed-out world, and to learn to notice and describe experiences. You'll develop an appreciation for what therapists call "time off the autopilot." Learning how to be more present takes time, but it all just boils down to practice, practice, and more practice—which we can do every day. Every day we do activities that become part of our routine. With just a little tweaking, I am sure we can add some mindfulness skills into that routine. Mindfulness will help you to step back and look at the bigger picture. This enables you to use your Pause button and ultimately make better decisions.

There Is Nothing Wrong with Thinking and Having Feelings

You may think, quite logically, that *all* negative emotions are unhelpful, but this isn't the case. Some can be really helpful. To illustrate this, let's look at Susie. She has suffered from an anxiety disorder called health anxiety for many years and altogether has experienced three separate episodes of health anxiety. Now she has learned more about how other emotions play a part in her problem, like sadness, shame, anger, and anxiety.

Previously, she would jump to the conclusion that, if she felt concern, she must be still have a problem. This would cause her to then spiral down very quickly. Mindfulness helped her see it for what it is—CONCERN! Susie now realises that it's OK to be concerned if a friend is not around this weekend or when saying good-bye to friends.

Think of your mind as a motorway. You are standing on an overpass, looking down at all the cars driving by underneath. The cars are your "worry thoughts," and at peak activity times, there are more of them—they're traffic and they block things up. At off-peak times, when you're relaxed, it's quiet and manageable. The overpass represents where you intend to go or what you intend to try doing. Think of yourself walking across that bridge and allowing the cars to run past underneath—this is what motorways are designed to do. The far end of the bridge can be anything: getting up, having a shower, meeting a friend, or tackling something that needs doing.

Fact Corner: Scientists believe that 70,000 thoughts pass through our minds daily. It's impossible to process each one, so you need to let many thoughts run through your mind unchecked.

Pit Stop Exercise: Close your eyes and look at the many thoughts running along the motorway in your mind. Describe the speed of the thoughts—are some slow and some fast? Does your mind try to block some thoughts? Does the mind use a stop-and-search policy?

Many people are tempted to try and stop most of the cars to search inside them, but this takes time and effort and yields little reward. Meanwhile, it keeps you from walking over to the far side of the bridge. Now, with a real motorway, you would never be able to stop more than a few cars! Why do this with your thoughts? Not every thought needs to be stopped and searched; let some just roll on by.

———•———

Pit Stop Exercise: Close your eyes and focus on your breathing. What do you notice? Describe any sensations you feel, i.e. the chest rising with every breath in and the chest falling with every breath out. Then, listen closely to sounds in the room. What can you hear? What do you notice? Describe what you notice. Do this for three minutes.

———•———

Fig 3.1 Practice form

Record on this page each time you practice the exercise above and make notes on what your experience is each time. What did you notice? Describe any sensations or observations.

Mini Practice form inside book

Date	Comments
02/02/2014 body scan	I noticed that I became more irritable when in the stomach area. I did not stay with. I wanted it to end

Don't Take Your Thoughts Personally

Do you take every thought that pops into your head seriously? If so, you'll need to learn to let them pass through. Our minds are full of thoughts, urges, actions, emotions, and sensations. We human beings are complex—we make many decisions in a split second based on intuition. To stop every single thought for analysis would make us simplistic creatures, and we are not simplistic.

Enjoy the fact that you are a fallible human being. Not to mention COMPLICATED! As human beings, we have many sides, facets, and experiences. We can and do make mistakes. The internal world of our thoughts is complex. We have both conscious and unconscious thoughts, of course, so let's focus on the thoughts that are in the here and now—life can be full with just those. Is it worth time and energy looking into the "coulda, shoulda and woulda's"? Or looking into the future thinking of "what if this?" "what if that?" If you hold every thought to be worthy of consideration, then you will quickly become exhausted and tired. Magical thinking in particular is one type of thought that soaks up a lot of energy. This includes telling ourselves statements like "if I say it then it will happen," "thinking it means I am bad," "people have said it so it must be true." Why is it that we always believe the bad ones and distrust the good ones?

———

Pit Stop Exercise: Buy a lotto ticket and use your magical thinking! Let's try and believe with all your might that you are the winner!

———

Now, magical thinking would have us believe that this will come true. But it doesn't. If we all did buy a lotto ticket and all believed with all our being then that there would not be any millionaires, right? Stop with the magical thinking. You are NOT your thoughts. You are not mad, bad, or dangerous. You are alive! Let's not judge our experiences through a lens of what makes us all good or makes us all bad. The simple truth is that you are alive and plugged into the matrix that is experience—enjoy!

A day in the life of a Therapist – the human condition: I was on the plane recently sat next to the exit door on the right side and middle of the plane, I choose this location for the extra leg room. Just waiting for take off and my mind decided to take me for a roller coaster ride with my attention caught up with the emergency lever and then "What if I pulled it?" which made me laugh a little to myself but then when the stewards did all the safety checks ready for the flight my brain went into the second roller coaster ride. The plane had just took off and the stewards were going through the health and safety procedure for passengers when my mind said "go on pull it" "the whole plane will dive" and the urge was so great to pull it that I had the tendency to act to neutralise my anxiety by sitting on my hands but then I remembered all my patients as if sat in front of me looking with disapproval and so I changed and I chose not to and instead played with the notion by pretending to yawn and stretch my arms out near to lever and then leave them there looking as if I was having a good old stretch.

Guess what nothing happened and passengers arrived safely at destination, but it occurred to me that all my work with OCD is beginning to rub off on me and that I ought to reduce my work load. That is one option but the other which sits more comfortably with me is to just understand that the mind has a 101 plus thoughts which are a mixture of good, mad, bad and dangerous but its passing traffic. Not every thought is fact, and indeed in one day the creative mind can pick up many stimulations via advertisements, colours, themes, ideas, words and emotions to name a few in any given moment. Think of the mind as a little black box, which are found on air craft, the box is used to collect data about the build up to a crash. If the mind collects data but then attach the criterion to it that would create and maintain OCD then life as you know it will start to reduce. But if another criterion is placed on it then maybe life will improve and the quality of it better

The mind is not always useful and so my reaction after my experiment was to laugh at myself for being so fearful in the beginning "there it is again my bloody mind.....thanks for that mind I really needed it.......NOT!

Discovering the Breath

Breathing is the most constant and consistent experience you and I have. Even if you suffer from irregular breathing, it will still be consistently irregular. It's a constant for all of us.

Pit Stop Exercise: Close your eyes and focus on your breathing. Reflect on how you are in control of the breath now, but you are not in control of the breath that has just gone—that is in the past—and neither are you in control of the breath to come—that is in the future. You are only in control of the breath NOW. Breathe in.

Breath is the very essence of living. Let's be in awe of the breath, and as you breathe in, envision it filling every part of your being.

Meditations to Start

These mediations will help you start your journey of recovery. Being able to think clearly will help you begin to feel better almost immediately.

Meditation Using the Eyes: I want you to open and close your eyes very slowly. Start from a squint, then relax the muscles around your eyes gently and very, very slowly. Begin to open your eyes fully, and then close them again as slowly as you can manage, eventually returning to the squint.

Meditation Using the Mouth: I want you to do the same with your mouth as you just did with your eyes. Slowly open your mouth until you stretch it as wide as is possible and then very slowly close it again until your lips are close together. Repeat until you feel a sense of calm and peacefulness.

Attention-Training Exercise: Keep your eyes focused on an object, then pay attention to the first sound you hear. What have you noticed? Describe it simply. For instance, "I can hear a ticking clock and the sound it makes is a tick-tock sound." Now move to sound two for a moment, and then move to sound three. The aim is to focus on three sounds over the course of three minutes. If a sound you focus on disappears, then focus on another sound that will last for the duration. Once you have heard all three sounds, listen to them all at once for a moment. Then returning to listening to them one at a time again for a second cycle.

Mindfulness of the Breath: Make sure you are seated comfortably, with your spine straight. Now focus on the belly. For the full duration of each inward breath and outward breath, focus on its movement of the belly. If your mind wanders many times, gently remind it to come back to the belly. Many distractions and preoccupations may pop into your head, but say "I will return to that later," and then focus on the belly again. Do this exercise for three minutes. Try to build up to ten minutes daily. Research shows that doing this simple exercise for ten minutes daily for six weeks can significantly change a pessimistic stance on yourself, others, and the world to an optimistic one.

Meditation in Action: This is about doing a simple task in slow motion and paying attention to the movement, sensations, and senses it creates. Many people choose to do this while brushing their teeth, for example. Really taste and smell the toothpaste.

How does your mouth react to the taste of toothpaste? Let a task that takes two minutes normally last for many more.

Sitting with Sounds: Wherever you are, just sit back and listen to what is going on around you. What sounds do you hear? Describe the sounds. Do you notice a difference when describing them with or without judgment?

Sitting with Thoughts and Feelings: Imagine that your mind is like a cinema screen. Your thoughts and feelings are displayed on it, in front of you. Now take time to notice how they present themselves. Do they pop up, or do they seep in from the edges, flooding your mind? Do crash over the screen as waves, or is it like a desert—is nothing there? How does your mind react when they arrive? Does the mind try to draw a curtain over them, push them to the edges of the screen, or just simply watch them passively?

Sitting with Choiceless Awareness: This meditation is about not focusing on anything in particular, but everything in general. Try to observe whatever attracts your attention or pops into your mind, and then, after a moment, move onto the next event to observe and so on.

Who Is Breathing?

Breathing is automatic, so it's easily taken for granted. Stop and look in the mirror at who is breathing? YOU. Let's get back to basics and focus on you. Start on your journey by acknowledging that you are the ONE who is breathing. Do you get anxious and hold your breath in fear? Remind yourself to breathe in the normal and natural way if you find yourself altering your breath's normal rhythm.

From Vulnerability Comes Creativity and Personality

Let's dispel the societal myth that equates being strong with not showing any weakness! This is wrong—strength comes from developing emotional muscle, and muscles can only be developed if exercised. True strength is about being honest and authentic. Feeling tested and vulnerable gives us a good workout.

Vulnerability is the one thing that many cultures around the world tell us to keep hidden. And yet this is the key to innovation, creativity, and change. Change cannot happen without the possibility of being vulnerable and allowing yourself to make mistakes. Many successful people have made many mistakes along the way—their secret is that they are not scared off by failure.

Motto: It's not what you do at the time that counts, but what you do after that matters. It's easy to stay hidden or to try and cover up a mistake. Try instead to come out from the shadows and be a little more transparent.

The emotion of shame is common among people who experience anxiety, depression, eating disorders, suicidal thoughts, violent tendencies, and addictions. It thrives on secrecy, judgment, and silence. The person believes that he or she is "damaged goods" or asks him or herself "who do you think you are?" Telling oneself "I am not good enough" stops many in their tracks. The antidote to shame is simply empathy. Tell someone: "I have felt that way, too!" Take a risk by attempting to connect with someone else. It will help you come out of the shame closet.

When combined with vulnerability, empathy brings people together who once were separated by silence, judgment, and secrecy. Empathy involves showing our humanity, and in the moment when we do, a connection takes place with another person. It takes courage to show vulnerability. Once you do, then your personality will shine through and you will not be locked up in shame's prison any longer. Instead, you will be ready to say, "I am here and here I stay, warts and all!"

Cultivating Strength and Smashing Shame

A famous biblical saying is "There is a time for joy, there is a time for tears, there is a time for sadness, there is a time for happiness." The saying goes on, but you get the message. When we are born, no one promises us that life will be fair and good all the time. We are like diamonds, moulded under pressure over time.

Experiencing life's pressures will bring about strength. And with experience comes a flexible mind. If we have a rigid mindset that cannot not see alternate ways of doing things, we will limit ourselves and ultimately keep ourselves from being successful. Flexibility is strength. Letting the mind entertain new and different ways of doing things along the journey of life is one of the key components of happiness.

Whenever you have a shame-based thought, ask yourself some questions about it. For example, "I must not let others see the true me because if they do, they will reject me."

1) How does thinking this help my mind behave in a rigid way?
2) What are the advantages and disadvantages of believing this so rigidly?
3) Is this thought helping me achieve my goals?

Take aging as an example. Some people have rigid views on how one should behave and dress at certain ages and believe that to do otherwise is shameful; others are open to new ideas and enjoy breaking the mould that society has placed upon them. Which group is enjoying life more? I think the group open to new ways of doing things, showing creativity and personality along the way.

Moment by Moment

"Being in the moment" is the catchphrase of the day lately, isn't it? But let's look at what it really means, as it is powerful. The ability to harness the moment starts with using some of your five senses—sight, hearing, touch, taste, and smell—in a situation.

Pit Stop Exercise: Put this book down for a moment and look around. What do you notice when you use each of your senses in turn? Look, smell, listen, taste, and touch? Describe it. Allowing yourself to truly "be in the moment" takes a risk, as it means you have to put on hold your brooding, worry cycle, complaining, plotting, setting yourself traps, etc. It takes a commitment to focus on something besides your usual concerns. Try it now. STOP the brooding about "coulda, shoulda, woulda's" and the worry cycle of "what if" and commit to the action for three minutes. Develop a curiosity about what is going on around you. Experience it as if you are a alien from another planet and you have just landed! What do you notice and enjoy?

The Way of Awareness

The pace of life is busier than ever. It is amazing that we can even cope with the complexity of our modern lives using just our intuition to make most of our everyday decisions. Remember that intuition is on your side. If you have not been listening to it, then take time to do so. We will explore this more in the next chapter.

Imagine for one moment walking through my clinic. You would see some people lying down and others sitting with their eyes closed, still. It may appear we are doing nothing. You would be right, if you consider our external actions, but inside something *is* happening. It's harder to stop and do nothing than you might think at first. Being in the moment takes work.

Notice I do not use the term "living for the moment," which has a different connotation to do with experiencing as much as possible as often as possible. I am concerned with helping people learn to slow down, to connect with themselves and others, and to practice simply "being." It helps the body to rest and have some down time. Make a commitment today to make time in your schedule of "doing" to practice at "being." Keep your eyes closed for ten minutes once a day. Connect to the now.

CHAPTER 4

Understanding the Brain and Thought Processes

In This Chapter You Will

- ◆ Learn the truth about how we make decisions
- ◆ Learn how knowing your emotions will help you make decisions
- ◆ Learn to enjoy the party and recover from anxiety

When addressing the subject of emotions, most people fall into two camps. Some people are OK with experiencing emotions, others are confused or scared by them. The latter group attaches many meanings to the experience of feeling strong emotions, and uses strategies like blocking to keep them at a distance. But a vast and rich life awaits those who can come to grips with and understand why emotions are important to us all. Embracing them as part of the menu of life will enrich you and those around you.

Understanding How Your Brain Makes Decisions

Understanding your emotions is a lifetime's work, but you can make a great start by investigating the possible explanations for *why* you experience them. For many years now, scientists have been researching the why and the following two sections explore what they have found. We'll look at the part of the brain responsible for making decisions as having two systems.

Meeting System One: Your Intuition

Our intuition is superfast, helps us save energy by offering instant responses to many things that we encounter in everyday living, and makes us experts at multitasking and at completing tasks with the least amount of effort required. In some cases, reasoning backs this up—see the following section. When the two work in tandem, we make the best decisions. Psychotherapists have found that people who acknowledge the experience of having emotions are better at making decisions than those who try to avoid or repress the experience of having emotions.

Spend a few moments now sitting and making a note of what emotions you are feeling today. Some common emotions are: sadness, concern, guilt, anger, annoyance, jealousy, envy, bitterness, hurt, sorrow, regret, embarrassment, shame, and low mood. Feel free to add others to the list or to use your own words.

———

> *Pit Stop Exercise: Spend five minutes noting what emotions you have felt today or are feeling now. Rate their intensity, where ten is most intense and zero is not intense. This will help you to make sense of your forest of emotions and thoughts. You will have knowledge about which you feel most keenly, and with knowledge comes power to make a change.*

———

If you are a person who has been described by others as "emotionless," don't fret. You can develop them over time by sitting with them for short periods and challenging yourself to experience them in a venue where you won't be overwhelmed by them. It's like building muscles in the gym—each time you add more weight, your body develops bigger muscles. It's the same with emotions. You develop them by gradually dealing with heavier and heavier ones. The end goal of acknowledging your emotions is about staying longer with them and being able to "sit comfortably in your own skin."

Motto: Keep it challenging but not overwhelming.

Meeting System Two: Your Reasoning

Reasoning helps us learn new skills. If you want to learn to fix an engine, for example, it may necessitate reading a manual. This process is slow and inefficient, as you need to keep going back and forth to the manual to learn. But as time goes by, then the skill becomes engrained. Eventually, you'll find yourself able to do it quickly. The knowledge that you have taken pains to acquire also becomes available to System One. System One taps into the vast experience and resources that you have to help you complete a task in an instant.

Mindfulness can help with intuition. From time to time, you might fall into bouts of negative thinking due to experiencing a sequence of stressful events. These can quickly spiral down into "I am bad, mad, and rubbish" thinking, which disturbs System Two's ability to reason. This also stops your ability to listen to your intuition, but mindfulness will allow you to step back and look rationally at the many emotions and thoughts you are experiencing whilst maintaining a connection to your intuition.

Using Mindfulness to Help You Look at the Bigger Picture

Mindfulness helps you to look at the bigger picture of how intuition and reasoning work together. It also helps you step away from unhelpful thinking patterns System Two might generate, or at least help you learn how not to take them at face value. Imagine viewing your thoughts and feelings up close in a mirror, so close your face is pressing against it. It may feel intense, difficult to manage, if so, then imagine looking at them from across a road—does the distance help with managing the thoughts or feelings? The answer is likely to be yes. Many have experienced the benefits of observing an experience as if from afar—you could also simply remind yourself that you are seated and that you don't need to act on it. Simply let it pass by.

Pit Stop Exercise: Write down a difficult thought or feeling that consumes you on a note pad and hold it up close, touching your face.

Ask yourself these questions:
1) *Where is your attention now?*
2) *What can you see?*

Then move the note pad out at arm's length or place it on your lap and then ask yourself the same questions. Compare and contrast the experience.

Diagnosis Corner: Some people associate meditation with the hippies back in the 1970s, but people from all walks of life practice it today. A definition of meditation is the practice of focusing on sounds, objects, sensations, tastes, smells, and visualizations in order to increase awareness of the present moment. We have all done this to some degree—like holding a newborn baby and then recalling the experience with warmth.

Fig. 4.1 A simple model of Anxiety

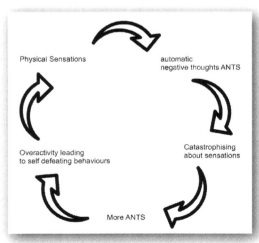

Focusing on four areas in this model can lead to a treatment plan: negative thoughts, brooding/worrying, isolation, and inactivity. Use the tool kit in this book to tackle each problem area. It takes courage to challenge an illness like anxiety. Remember to keep it simple and take small steps on the road to recovery.

Do You Have Intruders? Taking Care of Obsessive Thoughts

Gate-crashers may arrive at a party at any point, but do you spend your time barricading the door instead of enjoying the party? This is what obsessive thoughts are like: they always make you miss the party because you're trying to be so vigilant about trying to stop unwanted, intrusive thoughts from popping in for a visit. Many start by using the avoidance behaviour of thought, blocking these thoughts out of their minds, then proceeding to more improved ways of controlling the thoughts and images.

Blocking thoughts is a starting point. Ideally, you'll learn other mental rituals to help you neutralise anxiety like counting, tapping, reviewing events, and carrying out a postmortem on them to see if you did anything bad, mad, or dangerous. The core issue with obsessive thoughts is important to address here, as it becomes the central reason why compulsions and rituals are carried out. Did the reason start off being about making sure that you are not a bad person? Mad person? Or a dangerous person? If so, it makes sense that you would carry out such tasks to neutralise the anxiety—it makes you feel better. With a problem like Obsessive-Compulsive Disorder (OCD), this is a problem that defaults to low self-esteem. Every intrusive thought or image is controlled and managed. Remember that core beliefs are about self-esteem and begin with "I am" statements.

Examples

* I am weak.
* I am unlovable.
* I am a failure.
* I am crazy.

Its exhausting to constantly be on guard for thoughts and images that pop into the mind. Here is the thing to bear in mind: our brains are laid out like maps to transmit thoughts, images, and feelings just like a motorway is designed to carry cars of all shapes and sizes.

"Let's Enjoy the Party" as the Way to Recovery

Let's imagine your mind is like a party that many guests are attending. The aim is for you to learn to sit down and to spend time and attention on your guests. They represent your thoughts, friends, family, and all the Ideas for Living that are important to you. This can be hard work, but it is possible to direct your attention; you just have to learn to see that you can take your eyes off the threat of a party crasher. Learn to let go.

———

Pit Stop Exercise: Rate your mood right now out of ten, ten being bright in mood and zero being low in mood. Then think about obsessive or horrible, anxiety or depressive thoughts with the view of bringing your mood down for two to five minutes. Rate your mood again and then do the attention-training exercise where you listen to sounds. Listen to sound one for a while, and then move to sound two and so on with all three sounds. Remember, if a sound disappears, then find another sound. Listen to all three sounds together for a while, then listen to them separately again. Repeat this exercise a few times. Rate your mood again. Your mood should be back up to what it was initially. I hope this shows how you can direct your attention and change your mood even in a short space of time. This skill is particularly useful if you find yourself awake at midnight, struck by an anxiety episode.

———

My hope is that you will be able to enjoy the party by leaving the door unattended. You'll even allow the gate-crashers to come in but continue eating your cucumber sandwiches and drinking the Pimm's and chatting with some of your guests. When you can do this, you will have learnt to let go, to be able to live spontaneously and in the moment, trusting that you are a good person who makes mistakes occasionally. When you feel and know this intuitively, then you are seated in the party and spending time on what is important to you, not wasting time on the anxiety or obsessive thoughts.

——•——

Pit Stop Exercise: Try and consider how mad, bad, or dangerous you would really be if you were to allow some of your rules to be broken. Would it really mean the end of your world? Or would the world still go on? Having rules is fine, but can't they be broken sometimes? Also, can relationships with others really be less important that your views on contamination, order, symmetry, deviancy etc.? In OCD, many problems are associated with shame. Know that you have nothing to be ashamed of; and know that a preoccupation about keeping yourself away from others for fear of "harming" them seems altruistic but ultimately causes others to suffer as you isolate yourself from them. Check out some of your behaviours and see are you bad or dangerous by carrying out a task? Or is it the anxiety that makes it bad? If its anxiety then just get wet and surf the wave, if you fall off the surfing board you can swim!

——•——

Using Negative Thoughts to Your Advantage

Let me introduce to you a model that illustrates what I call the TRAP: Trigger-Response-Avoidance-Pattern. From the example below, you can see how avoidance can be subtle at first but, over time, it can develop into an established pattern of behaviour that reduces your overall quality of life. The alternative action is to follow a TRAC: Trigger-Response-And-Coping. This strategy helps you look for different possible outcomes to a situation than you would routinely select. It can be as simple as asking another colleague to lunch, or going to a restaurant you've never tried before alone with a tap on the back for simply having a go at trying something new.

Fig 4.2 The sequence of an event T. R. A. P.

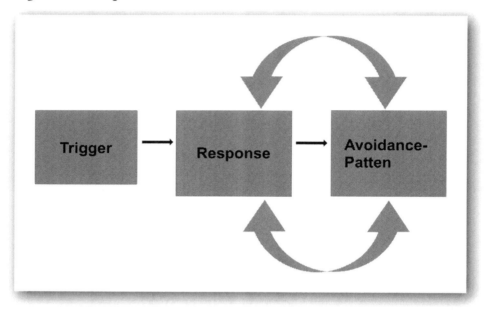

You Are Not Your Thoughts—This Isn't a Fusion Thing

On average, we experience 70,000 thoughts—on both conscious and unconscious levels—daily passing through without attaching meaning or fusing with them. If you were fused with your thoughts, then there would be 70,000 different fusions going on daily. Just thinking about that is enough to make *me* crazy. Most of these are just traffic. They're part of us, but what will help here is to simply be mindful of the fact that you can be slightly more obsessive than the average person and that is OK, but step away from that obsessive task or ritual and live according to your IFLs.

Beating, Brooding, and Worrying

It's important to optimise your ability to be in the moment so that you can focus on the challenges in front of you today. The problem with brooding and worrying cycles of thinking is that they happen when you are in avoidance mode. If you find yourself brooding or worrying, it's important to find out why. Psychotherapists call this the function of behaviour.

> *Motto: It's not what you do but why you do it.*

Avoiding Action

Can you think of any ways in which you avoid action because you brood or worry about the following areas?

a)   Family/relationships
b)   Social life
c)   Education/work
d)   Personal health
e)   Other

For some people, the function of brooding is to direct anger towards a perceived perpetrator. These people revisit events over and over in their minds, and try to tell themselves what they would say to the perpetrator if they could recreate the scene. For others, brooding has roots in shame; they relive the horror of a shameful situation, for example a time when embarrassing information about them was shared publicly or in a humiliating way. These are just two examples, but there are many more. The key here is to discover what emotion is driving the brooding/worrying response and then exploring the thought process behind that emotion.

Motto: When you're thinking that, what are you feeling? And vice versa.

I must also address the issue of boredom. As a race of people, we find it challenging to just sit, comfortably and in our own skin. Brooding and worrying can fill many voids. Being able to avoid boredom is important, as boredom can lead to many self-defeating behaviours, like excessive drinking of alcohol. It's OK to be quiet and maybe even enjoy sitting completely still. The mind does not need to be on duty all the time, and neither do you. Be off duty for a few hours—go on, try it once!

Recognising Opportunities

Once you are able to capitalise on being in the present, you will see opportunities where you did not before. You will also be able to take your life in directions that you had not thought possible.

Therapy Made A Difference—The Human Condition: A client called Sonia had been living with anxiety for twenty years. She had been seeing a therapist for ten years, but with no real results. Now, with CBT and MBCT, she has reduced her avoidance patterns of behaviour. One example of a therapy task was for her to focus on the anxiety sensations in her body and stay with these for as long as she was able to and by doing this the mind became desensitised and was no longer acting like a rabbit stuck in headlights. She has taken the risk to do something different and recognised that her ingrained ways of doing things were not set in stone. She changed, and so can you. You can train yourself to see possibilities and, after all, aren't you worth the effort?!

Taking an Interest in Life

Are there hobbies, interests, or jobs that you would like to pursue? Maybe things that you used to do or things that you would like to try but never had the chance? Write them down and see which one is most doable. Start. Remember, the UK has an aging population: 50 percent of us are fifty or older. So there will be a lot of time to fill in retirement, as more and more of us are now reaching the grand age of one hundred years. You could even have two or three different careers in that time. Decide to live the life that you want to live, rather than the life your parents had.

Keeping SMART

Remember to set goals that attainable and help you feel a sense of moving forward

S - specific, significant, small
M - measurable, meaningful, motivational
A - agreed upon, attainable, achievable, acceptable
R - realistic, relevant, reasonable, rewarding, results-oriented
T - time-based, time-bound, timely, tangible, trackable

CHAPTER 5

Examining Your Emotions

In This Chapter You Will

- ◆ Learn how describing your emotions can anchor you
- ◆ Take responsibility for finding the best way forward—for you
- ◆ Learn that there is nothing wrong with shame

Anxiety manifests itself in three interlinked domains: in thoughts, in feelings, and in behaviours. Feelings can be the most tricky to help treat, if only because feelings can be powerfully overwhelming. With all emotions it's about tolerance, tolerance, tolerance! Therapy on the whole is about learning to tolerate what once seemed intolerable. Remember, you can open the door and welcome all of your emotions in—even with a smile! This chapter helps you to develop knowledge about your emotions. When you understand them, you're halfway to dealing appropriately with them. The other half of the journey is recognising the message that specific emotions hold for you and using this message to improve your life. This process involves understanding the thought/feeling connection. By changing the way you think and how you respond to your emotions, you can become comfortable at experiencing any human emotion and using it in a positive manner—perhaps for personal change and growth or to motivate you to do something different in your life.

There Are Many Emotions in the Warehouse Called Anxiety

Yes you heard it right, I am calling Anxiety "the Warehouse." Anxiety can be accompanied by many emotions, like shame, anger, anxiety, hurt and low mood. All also interact in the condition of depression.

> *Pause: Depression does not just pop up from nowhere, it usually creeps up on us. This is what I call the life-shrinkage model. When you feel anxious, for example, you might avoid meeting up with friends, stop going to work, or make excuses to avoid feeling the anxiety. Then life as you know it shrinks away from you and you are left with a lot of losses. At this point, many automatic negative thoughts begin nagging at you and reminding you of the facts.*

Let me show you how using the idea of the warehouse will help you. In a warehouse, there are many parcels. It's your job to open these parcels one by one—you can't move them all at once. You may be experiencing all five of the most common emotions people report feeling during your anxiety, too, or just one or two. Choose an exercise from below linked to the emotion you feel to aid you in your recovery.

> *Motto: Keep it challenging but not overwhelming. You're human after all, not a superhero.*

Exploring Shame

The emotion of shame is one that people from all different societies and cultures battle. In many countries, if a young women is raped, for example, instead of punishing the rapist sometimes the family is shamed into forcing their daughter to marry the rapist. Shame forces the family to act in an unnatural way to maintain the social currency of family honor.

Shame is also prevalent in UK. As recently as the 1960s, for example, unwed mothers would be forced to give up their children to the government and, unbeknownst to the mothers, their children be shipped away to another country so no one would know or find out. But even Australia was not far enough, it turns out, and the silence surrounding this secret policy has now finally been broken.

Let me show you some common thoughts associated with shame. When the mind experiences shame, it will tell you things like:

- Who do you think you are?
- You're not good enough.
- Others will find out how bad you are.
- Everyone will see you fall.

Shame flourishes and thrives in the dark. The antidote to shame is empathy. To blast it away, you must break the silence and secrecy surrounding it. The sense of judgment shame makes us feel is deep and heavy, and it takes away joy from you on a daily basis. But by "coming out" and declaring to the world "I am here and I have a right to live the life that I was born to live!!" many people have experienced a lightening of the load.

Shame grows when these three ingredients are present:

- Secrecy
- Silence
- Judgment

Nelson Mandela said that no single population of people is in possession of the full truth. He suggested we unite to bring the strands of truth each group possesses together to benefit all. But first, of course, the truth needs to be out in the light. Are you living true to yourself?

Are you a gay man struggling in silence and pretending to be a straight man, even going so far as to marry a woman instead of a man? Are you a victim of abuse who has not shared that devastating history with someone close to you? Or are you a perpetrator of violence, beating up your wife or husband and trying to get rid of the feeling of shame that causes you by hitting him or her even more?

I would like you to take a risk. Tell someone close to you why you feel ashamed. Rid yourself of the three deadly ingredients of shame. Your reason for feeling ashamed may not be as serious as the issues listed above, but your sense of shame may still be strong. Be courageous and tell someone.

Being empathetic means putting yourself in the position of trying to understand someone else's pain, offering statements like "me too," or being able to imagine walking in another person's shoes. Sympathy is slightly different—it's to show concern but not to fully feel someone else's pain as it has not happened to you. Both, however, are powerful expressions of love, caring, and attention that help us connect to other human beings.

Pit Stop Exercise: This week, why not try making a "me too" statement to someone who shares a secret with you? Measure how much this affects your mood on a scale of 0/10 where 10 = bright in mood and 0 = low in mood. What happened to your mood after that exchange? If it had a positive impact, consider doing it again in another situation. Being courageous means owning up to your vulnerabilities.

Fig 5.1 The Shame Attack Exercise

Pit Stop Exercise: This is a great exercise to help you to overcome self-consciousness, social embarrassment, and inhibitions. The point of the exercise is to create an experiment, that is designed to forcefully and directly challenge your sense of shame. So for example, if you have a sense of shame about acting inappropriately in public, then go and do something mad in public repeatedly. For instance, you might shout out the individual tube stops as the train pulls into them along the full length of the Victoria Line. The idea here is to train yourself to feel sorry for what you did, but not to put yourself down or to feel humiliated about your personhood. Many people feel a sense of empowerment and almost become giddy with a huge sense of achievement after trying similar exercises, as if a weight was taken off their shoulders.

Assessing Anger

Life-shrinkage often leads to being angry with yourself. The anger can stem from things that have been done to you or with you, but if left to grow anger can be just as crippling as shame because of its ability to isolate us from others. Some people would say that annoyance is a good term to use for healthy anger but constantly thinking about a sin committed is unhealthy anger.

> *Motto: It's not what you do, but why you do it that counts.*

Sadly, I have come across many individuals who have isolated themselves because of an event that took place ten, twenty or even forty years earlier. When anger festers for this long, it turns to outright hatred. Brain scans have shown that when a person focuses on a moment of anger, the area of the brain that registers distress lights up strongly. When the participant is instructed to move his or her thoughts away from the angry situation and to think of the next thing they had to do that day or a bigger-picture theme, the distress no longer shows up on the scan.

Anger, like shame, leads to self-defeating behaviours like complaining, setting traps, punishing others and yourself or monitoring others. All of these require lots of energy, so they simply wear you out. The habits you have created to deal with your anger will take time to break, but it's your job to break them. The mindfulness meditations in this book are a good way to overcome just such destructive habits.

Some people tend to keep all their emotions inside. This causes us to use them in an angry way to punish ourselves. It is a good idea to consider taking the risk of having a conflict with someone else in order to voice your displeasure. This is almost always better than bottling up emotions. Check in with the other person to see if you understood them or their actions correctly first. This will at least start a dialogue. If his or her actions still make you feel angry after you've heard the explanation for them, you have given yourself the opportunity to say so. Telling someone else you disagree with them is not the end of the world; you won't spontaneously combust on the spot. Wondering about someone's motivation or replaying a disturbing event in your mind, however, is exhausting and drains your energy.

Remember, it's what the person has said that has made you angry—not the person him or herself. People are not all bad or all good, but a mixture of the two. We are all allowed to voice our opinions—and that includes you, too!

Fig 5.2 The Anger 4-Step
Top Tip for Dealing with Anger: The Four-Step Approach

1. **Walk away. Decide to come back to the situation in one hour, then make an excuse to walk away. Say, for example, that you need to make a call or say you are late for an appointment.**
2. **Get calm. Go for a slow walk or find another activity that you can do slowly.**
3. **Rethink. How do you want others to think about you? How do you want to think about yourself? Ask yourself if you are fostering/nurturing the relationship with yourself or the other person with your reactions.**
4. **Come back with a response. This can be a response to yourself, such as "I am annoyed about…but it's OK and life goes on." A response to another person might be "Let's agree to disagree," or "I am sorry."**

This approach was conceived to help you remember that hindsight is golden. It will keep you from thinking "I wish I had acted differently. If I could redo it, I would act like…"

Think of this four-step plan as a Pause button to use while you collect your thoughts and decide on a course of action. Thinking of your life on Rewind all the time can cause you to feel hot with anger, but Pause can help you see potential consequences before they occur and help you to salvage a situation before it becomes a problem.

Acknowledging Anxiety

Being generally anxious about things or being specifically anxious about one type of thing, like social gatherings or having intrusive thoughts/images, can set off a chain of events that lead to a reduction in your activities. Fear is one of the emotions that commonly causes life-shrinkage, because you make decisions one after another to cut out anxiety, but that leaves you with nothing left to experience.

If your solution to anxiety has been to cut people or activities out of your life, let me show you how your solution is the problem. Anxiety is processed in a part of the brain called the amygdala. When a feared situation occurs, like a real intruder breaking into my clinic, I will act instinctively by either running away or fighting the intruder. In a car crash, I will act instinctively and get out of the car as soon as possible after the collision.

In real-life situations, the amygdala acts quickly to release hormones that cause a chain reaction; its sole aim is to keep you safe. Adrenaline is released from the adrenal gland, just above the kidney, which causes your blood to pump super fast. Then a sugar-type substance is released and transported by the fast-moving blood to fuel all the muscle groups needed for a quick getaway or a fight for survival. This is why you feel many uncomfortable sensations when you are anxious or fearful. The butterflies or nausea in your stomach are due in part to the adrenaline being released.

Think about this chain reaction going on inside you the next time you are anxious. Our brains are wired to set it off, and the amygdala is there to keep you safe. It will react using the flight and fight mechanism—it's just not that good at deciphering what is a life-threatening situation and what is a self-inflicted feeling of anxiety, so it sets it off in either case.

But is it necessary to react to your intrusive thoughts in the same way as a real intruder or car crash? Remember that anxiety has its different levels of intensity from high intensity to low intensity abit like going up over a hill and down the other side. When running from a real intruder, the anxiety wears off very quickly—as soon as you escape—but the amygdala will remember the way you escaped and present it to you as an option to use again later. This means the same physical response is initiated for the imaginary intruders, your thoughts. When you enact a behaviour to keep yourself safe, it neutralises the feeling of anxiety but reinforces the problem. This will set up a pattern for the next time you are fearful.

Let me show you a case of someone who uses safety-seeking behaviours. Joe, who is overly sensitive in periods of anxiety, seeks reassurance constantly from his wife. She is exhausted by it. Joe will ask constantly if he has behaved OK or if he has upset the other members of the family. By getting the reassurance that he was fine, the anxiety disappears quickly. This forms a habit that the brain remembers, so it encourages Joe to keep asking in order to help him feeling safe.

Common safety-seeking behaviours that fuel problems are:

- Seeking reassurance
- Avoiding eye contact
- Sitting in corners away from people
- Sitting near exits
- Monitoring where the toilets are
- Never allowing for some flexibility and allowing others to have a different viewpoint

But the reassurance is the very problem. Joe is not actually able to ever be reassured. He is just stuck in a pattern of constantly needing to be topped up. Joe recognised that this behaviour maintains his cycle of anxiety. He now works conscientiously to face the idea of not seeking reassurance. He has learned to sit with the uncertainty of not knowing. Eventually this builds up "muscle" in his mind and helps him to recover.

Now, instead of using fight-or-flight behaviours, Joe visualises the anxiety as a rainshower. He has learned to let the anxiety wash over him like water in a shower—it's not the end of the world if he gets a little bit wet. The same principle can help you change your life. As you become less and less anxious, you'll become more courageous and will walk with your head held high.

———

Pit Stop Exercise: Try looking at your own safety-seeking behaviours. Decide which ones are flight behaviours and which are fight behaviours. This will be useful in helping you to understand how and why you use these functions, with a view to dropping the behaviours.

Angry Hurt

Feeling hurt can be a helpful emotion when it's related to disappointment. When relationships are strained, for example, one party gets disappointed with the other. You feel hurt, but it's up to you to determine whether this is the right time to something about it and bear the consequences. The main learning point about emotions is that they can lead to relationship richness if you stay in the moment with the other person and stay connected, authentic.

Angry hurt, however, causes a complete disconnect with the other person. People who are angry hurt will often dredge up or rant about old history, which leads to sulking behaviours like isolation.

Isolation may be a way to protect oneself, but it may also be used as a punishment for other people, as in when you remove your presence and leave a friend or relative alone. Punishing never really affects the other like you want it to—take it from me—so just quit it and get back to talking with them.

It's normal to get hurt. This is part of life. What's harmful is when you let an issue fester and you rant about it five years from now. The truth of the matter is: people forget. If you are disappointed but uncertain about whether to confront someone about his or her behavior, then ask yourself: is it worth rocking the boat?

Motto: If no, then let it go.

If yes, then say your piece while looking into the eyes of the other. At least you'll connect. Looking into the eyes helps you to be succinct and to get straight to the point.

Looking at Low Mood

Moods fluctuate due to a reduction in the happiness neurotransmitter, serotonin. The lower its level, the lower in mood you become. Its as if the brain goes through a shutting down process to keep you warm, save your energy, and reduce your higher-level functioning—but not to regenerate as you might think. Sometimes we rest and then feel rejuvenated again, but that is not what happens with depression. Instead, the brain simply gets used to not functioning in certain ways and goes through a process of deconditioning. This is a term used by psychotherapists to describe unlearning and reduced physical activity that leads to muscle loss. Heart muscle also atrophies during this time, making it difficult to resume old activities again. Your mood will get brighter when you do exercise, reengage with relationships, face some avoidance issues, and develop your relationship with YOU!

Chasing Your Tail!

We learn early on in most cultures not to show vulnerability or weakness of any kind in front of anybody. This is perceived, mistakenly, as a sign of strength. But this really does need to stop. When a person puts up a wall around him or herself, this is not a show of strength—it's a step towards loneliness and isolation. What would happen if you knocked down the wall? What would it mean to you to do this? It could be scary, but would it also bring benefits? Let me show you how to look at the potential benefits of just such a move as thought it were a simple cost-benefit analysis. This is a useful method of putting down on paper thoughts about a proposed action or a belief in an attitude.

Fig 5.3 Cost Benefit Analysis Form

Example of CBA

ADVANTAGES/BENEFITS OF the attitude: I must not feel anxious and I can't bear it

SHORT TERM – for yourself

1   I can keep myself safe
2   I don't do certain things
3   I have something to talk about

SHORT TERM – for other people

1 They can help me
2 They will do things I can't do therefore I am relieved
3

LONG TERM – for yourself

1   More keeping safe
2   More not doing things
3   People will know me as one knowledgeable about anxiety

LONG TERM – for other people

1 They will learn to cope without me
2 They will not rely on me therefore the pressure is off
3

DISADVANTAGES/BENEFITS OF the attitude: I must not feel anxious and I can't bear it

SHORT TERM – for yourself

1 No matter how often I tell myself that I should not feel it, the feeling is still there
2 The more rigidly I hold the attitude the more worse it gets
3

SHORT TERM – for other people

1 Others don't see me very often as I am stuck indoors
2 I cannot join new projects
3

LONG TERM – for yourself

1 My attitude are not consistent with my reality
2 Its interfering with my goals

LONG TERM – for other people

1 They learn not to include me and I will be isolated even more
2 They will not trust me as I am not around alot

Emotions Are Our Friends

I want you to imagine that your mind is like a party. All your favourite guests are there, but you are nowhere to be seen. Why? Because you want to stop the intruders—emotions—getting in by barricading the door. Let me show you that by barricading the door, your attention is taken up with the potential intruders and not the guests. If you treat emotions like intruders and you feel exhausted by them, it's time to try something new.

———

Pit Stop Exercise: Use your imagination now. Close your eyes, let the door go, and sit with your guests at the party in your mind. These guests are thoughts, actions, hobbies, interests, friends, family, work, etc. Be with them. Choose one to focus on and be with, and use your intuition to make some decisions. Allow yourself to let go of the door and walk towards that guest of choice.

———

Noticing, Describing, and Tolerating Your Feelings

The process of mindfulness requires you to notice, describe, and tolerate your feelings, but what does this really mean? I will show you by asking you to look at an object near you. Once you've selected it, please describe in your own words—i.e. I see a traditional wooden sun lounger from the 1950s era; it's made of thin wooden strips of wood with gaps in between; four points support it and it has two pieces of crossed wood underneath the seat area. Is there a negative judgment in that description? No. Describing without judging can be hard to do. We are used to putting a negative slant on everything in our modern era, and the world of social media especially encourages us to do this. Once you have tackled a few objects, repeat this exercise with the thoughts and feelings in your mind.

———

Pit Stop Exercise: Step back and look at the bigger picture by using your awareness. Sit down, keeping your spine straight, and focus on your belly. Breathe in as deeply as you can and out completely. If your mind wanders, gently bring your awareness back to your belly. Accept that your mind will wander but lead it back to your breathing. Now, what thoughts and feeling do you notice? Describe them impartially. You might say, for example, "I feel anxious and I have the sensation of butterflies in my stomach and tightness in my chest." Job done! Now move on to describe another whilst all the time focusing on your belly and breathing.

———

Stuck in a Cycle of Reacting to Stress Instead of Responding to It?

We human beings are remarkably resilient. We find many ways to cope with stress and to survive. We love life and use our interests, religion, family, community, and other diversions to feed our need to belonging to a social group. At the same time, we are capable of overstretching ourselves and pushing our bodies to the limit. This happens over a period of time as ingrained habits and coping strategies exacerbate our stress levels. Too much time spent at work and addictive behaviours lead to the breakdown of personal relationships and consequently to depression. *Reacting* is acting without thinking. *Responding*, however, is giving yourself a choice of two or more options. The latter enables self-empowerment and puts you back in the driver's seat.

Take a Look!

Stress can be a good thing when it motivates you to do better and develop confidence. So when a deadline looms, for example, we respond with a flurry of activity and then reward ourselves with down time when the body can rest and rejuvenate. Problems arise when the down time does not take place. Some people keep themselves in a constant state of heightened stress, and this has a negative impact on physical and mental health. Many who say that they have groomed themselves to be passive are really keeping what they think and feel inside and are hypervigilant about not revealing emotions—this is also an example of being in a permanent state of stress.

Unfortunately, humans don't have a safety valve. The body will adjust to the self-grooming if we train it to. We will go so far as developing a way of looking OK when in fact inside we are falling apart. Over years, living in a constant state of near-catastrophe becomes part of your nature, but it can easily lead to depression.

———————

Fig 5.4 Problem Solving Technique

Pit Stop Exercise: Write down a problem in one sentence. Then, in another sentence, write down the solution. Try not to write "Problem: I am stressed!" Try instead to be specific as possible like for instance, "Problem: I am not honest about how I feel when my partner asks me about moving house. Solution: Find time to talk openly with my partner and say I don't want to move but lets look at the options."

Often, when in a cycle of reacting to stress, we don't allow ourselves to respond and the cycle continues with lots of tears and heartache. By condensing your thoughts into one sentence, you can help yourself find a practical way out. Act on the solutions you find. Spend twenty minutes a day recording what you have found out about yourself by doing something new or by carrying out an exercise from this book.

———————

Change Is a Sure Thing

From the day you are born, your cells regenerate constantly. Change is part of the human condition. People move from one place to another to make a better life for themselves. If you are struggling with change, then maybe you also struggle with vulnerability and allowing others into your life. If you embrace vulnerability then change, innovation, and creativity will happen, boosting your life experience. A type of thinking that views change as a threat is what we call Low Frustration Tolerance (LFT), which is the type of thinking along the lines of "I can't bear it." This causes you to erect mental walls. Your mental checklist says that "I need all my boxes ticked before I can move ahead." This type of thinking leads to unhelpful stress and will leave you feeling stuck.

The opposite condition is known as High Frustration Tolerance (HFT). This requires changing the language you use to think about a problem to statements like "I can do it" and "I can sweat the small stuff and some big stuff." This comes with a different mental checklist, which might consist of saying "I don't need all my boxes ticked before I can move ahead, but I will step out on what I know now and find out as I go." Flexibility allows you to deal with what comes your way and still bounce back quickly. The rigid "I won't do…" attitude leads to more stress and high probability of negative repercussions.

To develop HFT, try doing something new that takes you out of your comfort zone. Ask for help. Show you are human by acknowledging that you do not know it all—and neither do you believe you have to know it. Just do it. You will feel better as your confidence in that task gets better.

Fig 5.5 Ideas for developing HFT

> *Top Tips for Developing High Frustration Tolerance*
> *Say hello to someone new. Try saying the first thing that pops into your head at a social gathering. Help someone even when you don't feel like it. Accept help from someone even when you don't feel like it. Spend an extra thirty minutes exercising. Don't say "I can't" but instead say "I can do it!"*

Listening to Your Body

There is a pill for every ache and pain. Adverts tell us the zap-it-and-be-gone attitude is the best, but this doesn't leave us a chance to wonder if in fact the body could be trying to tell us something. Accepting a process where we allow symptoms to show us how to accept ourselves in the moment, right now, as we are—in pain or not in pain, fearful or not fearful—can teach us much about our mental state.

The mind will often jump to what I call "the reject and eject mode," which is a false sense of security, often judgmental, fearful, and self-preoccupying. We would do better to ask: "What is the symptom saying?" "What does it tell me about my mind and body right now?" Allowing a symptom to continue bothering you takes courage, especially if the symptom involves a long-term condition like diabetes, after effects of a stroke, cancer, cardiac problems, etc.

Allow yourself to become aware of the feelings you have about the symptoms you experience. These may be anger, fear, or despair, to name but a few. Try dealing with these by remembering to be in observer mode.

———

Pit Stop Exercise: Imagine you're David Attenborough observing a landscape and the animals within it. These animals are your feelings, thoughts, urges, tendencies, and actions. What do you notice? E.g. Description: I feel butterflies in my stomach almost like anticipation of something. There is also a tendency to judge my experience as being unacceptable but I will not get onboard with that but just sit with it with a kindly attitude.

———

Working with Physical Pain

A large percentage of the population suffers physical pain. In the UK, one in three people attending a mental health service also reported suffering from pain relating to a long-term condition. Mindfulness is especially helpful with managing physical pain.

Let's look at a headache as an example. Your mind will develop thoughts and feelings surrounding the headache. The reject and eject mode wishes the body to have a different experience. It doesn't acknowledge that this headache may be part of something else. If you think about the headache in a larger context, however, you might ascertain whether it's related to a whole chain of events or another illness.

Also, are you able to just call it a headache, or is it a feeling in your head without a name? Wording is essential in our experience. Some will say "everything is a headache" to mean that they are anxious. Overgeneralization tends to lead to other problems and to be self-defeating.

Going on a Journey from Beginner Mind to Wise Mind

View your mind as a work in progress. It's is the best way to think about it. It's natural for your mind to jump around from one thing to another, but it's your job to bring your attention back to the movement of the belly when meditating. The beginner mind—a term used to refer to someone new to meditation—always needs to be preoccupied with the shopping list, TV schedule, what to wear, etc. This is because we have trained ourselves to be preoccupied. Technology gives us the ability to be always available, to find out knowledge about any subject in an instant, and to control our physical environment. Try a week without a mobile, a laptop, or a thermostat! The aim of meditation is not to learn to give up what we love, but to train the mind in a different direction with the view of disciplining it. Once stillness has been achieved, you are halfway to being in the wise mind.

Fig 5.6 Distress Tolerance Skill 1

> *Pit Stop Exercise: Dealing with Distress—Skill One*
> *Close your eyes and sit or lie down in a comfortable position. Begin breathing in and out. Spend some time now to get into a rhythm. Then turn your attention to how your body is feeling right now. Notice the position of your hands, arms, torso, bottom, legs, and feet. Observe using your senses; pay attention to the sounds you can hear in the room and describe them to yourself without judgment. Move your attention to sounds you can hear outside of the room. What do you notice? Describe it in a straightforward, factual way.*

E.g. "I can hear the clock ticking in the room, it sounds like a tick-tock sound." This is observing and describing what you notice.

Try the same again, but adding a judgment. See the difference it makes to experiment with your experience. E.g. "I can hear the clock ticking in the room. It sounds like a tick tock sound, which is infuriorating, and I want to put the clock in another room

———

Fig 5.7 Distress Tolerance Skill 2

Pit Stop Exercise: Dealing with Distress—Skill Two

Repeat Skill One and then move to this skill. Pay attention to sounds outside of the room, then move your attention to your thoughts. What do you notice? Describe what you notice.

It may be that the mind tries to block thoughts and images, or the mind may let them rush in and out. The mind will do something with your thoughts, however, and it is this that we need to discover.

Let's move your attention to your emotions or feelings and see how the mind reacts to or processes these. Do the feelings come as waves rushing in and out? Is it calm? Again, observe what the mind does with each feeling. Remember: you do not have to react or act on the feeling or thought. You are merely observing the feeling. Let's take time to remind yourself that you don't have to attempt to get rid of the thought or feeling. Some feelings can be intense and may lead to self-harming behaviour. Slow down and remember that you are just sitting quietly in a chair. Give yourself permission to stay there and not worry about how to deal with your emotions for the time being.

———

CHAPTER 6

Getting Motivated and Improving Self-Esteem

In This Chapter You Will

- Look at resilience and learn the right self-talk for success
- Decide if another approach is needed, like Unconditional Self-Acceptance
- Learn the definition of high self-esteem

This chapter will help you understand yourself and give you some perspective that will help you move forward. Let's first check out what psychotherapists mean by the term self-esteem. It refers to the evaluation of how we place emphasis on worth and how we rate ourselves to match that idea of worth. The problem with self-rating is that it works well when you're bright in mood but is disastrous when you're low in mood. The concept of Unconditional Self-Acceptance (USA) may prove more helpful with understanding self-esteem; it gets rid of the rating game and looks instead at acknowledging what we can do and what we cannot do. Accepting ourselves unconditionally develops compassion. Acceptance is not to be confused with self-resignation, however, or with being defeatist. Rather, think of the word "acknowledgment." Acceptance according to USA is about being able to notice and describe your experiences. In this chapter, I will show you how to develop self-acceptance with a side salad of compassion.

This will aid you in your recovery and help you to maintain your wellness longer.

Identifying Issues of Low Self-Worth

Low self-worth can come from negative early life experiences like abuse and bullying, but also it can come from the way we are wired. As human beings go, we have an innate ability to look to the negative. This is how we disturb ourselves, as we are always looking to where the grass is greener. This mechanism has its roots in survival—we are built to identify the best options since improving our lot means increased security, but this mechanism can also turn on itself. We can also use it to beat ourselves up. We all have the ability to self-destruct and to destroy others in the process. The evidence is all around on the global news—not forgetting on our own doorstep.

Wanting High Self-Esteem?

Many say "I suffer from low self-esteem," but I sometimes wonder if they know what they actually want to achieve. What does it mean to have "high" self-esteem? Here are some answers I hear repeated over and over:

- "I want to do well at work."
- "I want to be a good mother."
- "I want to live according to my principles."
- "I want to be in a loving relationship."

These all relate to being desirable and/or accomplished, but none of these necessarily raise self-esteem in the long term. What would happen if a relationship broke down or you lost a job? If your self-esteem hinged on those, it would be back down to the self-damning statements of "I am unlovable" or "I am a failure." These drain your energy and simply make you want to hide from everyone and go to bed.

This quest for high self-esteem can be fraught with problems; many who claim to have high self-esteem also say they experience high levels of anxiety and aggression. So let's aim for middle-of-the-road by looking at ourselves saying, "I am OK. I am alive and breathing the same air as everyone else." Use the mindfulness to notice the mental events of the mind and how the mind reacts to thoughts about self and its ability to accept self unconditionally

Questioning What You Really Want

Trying to be great and super at everything all the time is destructive—it's simply not possible because it's not the way we are built. Let's aim at just being OK and acknowledging that all of us are equal. We all are born and we all will die. Everything in between is what we do as part of the process of self-development. We can only self-actualise our potential within the resources we have available.

Avoiding Errors When Challenging Low Self-Worth

One of the most common boosts we use to raise our own self-esteem is putting others down. The problem with this is that it just aids in the eventual alienation of friends and family, which can further exacerbate anxiety.

Rather than looking at others and criticizing them, let's look to ourselves and get our positive data logs out. Let's spend some time acknowledging what we've got instead of trying to identify what others don't and being judgmental. Being judgmental is not an attractive quality when experienced in large doses

Thinking That You're Inferior

We have all felt inferior at one point or another. There is always someone who knows more than we do; but remember that others know less. The ability to keep this in mind comes with experience, but eventually you will be able to impart your knowledge and experience to someone who needs your help. Embrace this natural order of things and affirm to yourself that it's OK not to know everything about everything.

Feeling Superior

Feeling superior is the other side of the same coin as feeling inferior, but it is still a problem if you base your sense of self-worth on this idea. As a rule, people do not enjoy being around others who act superior. The group you are with will put you in your place once they sense your attitude. Try to slow down and "just be" with people. Showing off constantly to try and assert your superiority can be exhausting—both for you and the listener! Chill.

Believing That You're Special

The next obvious way to boost self-esteem is to talk yourself into believing that you're special. This is often related to a *need* to feel special; you can convince yourself that you're more essential than everyone else in some capacity, but it's a sure way to distance yourself from others.

Anthropology teaches us that we were once tribal beings who lived in villages where the community had a leader. Usually he/she would be a fierce warrior. All the tribe members, however, had a role within the community. No one person was more special than another; all had a social standing within the community and a job to do.

Spend some time now exploring your roles within your social circle and your jobs to do. Remind yourself of what they are and do them! The specialness routine will get picked up on the others' radar, and you could quickly be identified as the sticky wicket in your community. If you want to be part of a group, drop the act and just be yourself. You are fallible, others are fallible, and so is the rest of the world—you're in good company!

Trying to Control Other People

Attempting to control others to make you feel good about yourself and boost your self-esteem is also not advisable. This one grants no favours and will bite you on the back eventually. Controlling people don't have much respect for other people's thoughts, feelings, or experiences. Therefore, they become unattractive in other people's eyes. Friendships tend to suffer greatly with this one.

Seeking Approval

Approval-seeking behaviour is another way to boost our ego, but again it does not help you to become self-sufficient; it requires that someone else place a coin in your slot machine to keep you going. Be sustainable. Allow moments of disapproval to occur and learn from them. They are useful experiences. Like the fifteenth-century British monk John Lydgate once said, "you can please some of the people some of the time, but not all of the people all of the time."

Behaving Defensively

Defending self-worth is a sure sign of unhealthily high self-esteem. These people defend themselves with aggression, and research has shown that people who suffer from too high self-esteem have problems with anxiety and aggression, and therefore impact friends and family relationships negatively.

Being Specific

Blaming the past or other outside influences for your problems, which can temporarily boost your sense of self-worth, only camouflages the situation. It does not get you to change your self-damning thought pattern. This is not to negate the impact other people can have on your life experiences, but you are here, now, so breathe and reboot.

Responding and Not Reacting

Welcome to the human race. You're in good company! Many of us have experienced rejection, a difficult childhood, horrible bosses...the list goes on. Use compassion and understanding to make sense of your own past, and approach others with a warm, sympathetic, and empathetic perspective to help you move forward. Life as we know it will continue with or without our participation—empower yourself to make a healthy choice as to how *you* move forward and join in.

Spend time in responding to the present moment. If you don't enjoy your own company and react to every spook of negative thoughts or feelings, well, then that means that is the place to start. Go for a coffee with yourself and write up a list of things you would, might, or never like to do with yourself. Then get to it and do the first item on your "would like to do" list.

Knowing Yourself

Build a relationship with yourself. Try it and see—you might like it! There are bound to be parts of yourself that you don't like, but that is also true of some of your friends and family and you manage to love them. Is it possible to like some of the parts of your own person and to allow yourself to not like the other parts? I think it is.

This is the human experience: you, others, the world, and I are partly good, partly bad, and mostly indifferent. We all have made mistakes, and I am sure we will all continue to make them, too. Human beings are fallible. In fact, we are only certain of two things: death and taxes! The rest is up to you and I. Remember that we are all equal—we are all alive and breathing the same air.

Playing the Rating Game

Self-rating to make yourself feel worthwhile is a lost cause. It makes us place conditions on ourselves that, in turn, we can never live up to all the time. We are all a mixture of good and bad, able and unable. Let's just embrace it. Let's still evolve and improve our lives, but let's agree to ditch the self-damning talk. This will make life a lot easier and maybe help us achieve our goals.

Practicing Unconditional Acceptance

The concepts above may help you to place the idea of self-rating to one side, so let's take a look at what Unconditional Self-Acceptance, an idea that can take its place, offers. It looks at the bigger picture and acknowledges the whole self. Imagine for one moment that you are a big oil painting; you have to step back a few feet for the whole image to be seen, right? When your nose is pressed against the painting, you can only focus on one stroke of paint. Imagine also that all you happen to be able to see is one dark stroke of black paint. It's hard to see the beauty in such a small detail. To make matters worse, your head probably shadows the area you're trying to see, which makes the specific section of the painting you're focused on darker and bleaker.

Let's now evaluate how you look at failure and the darker areas of your life. Are you the one who has his or her nose pressed up against the picture? Try taking a step back to see the bigger picture.

There is more to you than you give yourself credit for, and the black paint or shadow on the painting might provide the painting with nuance or texture. Try to see how it works to make the whole a work of art. Step back and look at yourself in your entirety. You are made up of thoughts, feelings, and behaviours accumulated by living a lifetime with others—and by spending time alone. These help you carve out your unique place in the world. So now you see that it is virtually impossible to have one global rating justify all your experiences.

Appreciating That Unconditional Self-Acceptance Is the Key

We are wired to place conditions on ourselves. Try instead to do the exercise below, which aims to help you see how multifaceted you are. It is impossible to rate any one area over generalizing negative aspects to mean something horrible and damning. Accept that there may be specific moments of time when you will be bad, and leave it at that. Ask yourself only what the next moment will be—if good, then move out to greet it.

———

Fig 6.1 The Self-Acceptance Egg

Pit Stop: Looking at Yourself and Your Identity
  Draw an egg shape on a large piece of paper. The egg represents you. Answer these questions:

- Who are you? (These are your roles, like: I am a mother, I am a carer, etc.)
- What hobbies and interests do you like to do now?

- What are the positive personality traits that you like about your-self? (These are descriptions of yourself, like caring, kind, etc.)
- What are the negative personality traits that you dislike about yourself?
- What are the positive characteristics that you like about yourself? (These are your caring, kind behaviours for example.)
- What are the negative characteristics that you dislike about yourself?
- What are the thoughts about self that you like?
- What are the thoughts about self that you are ambivalent or neutral about?
- What the thoughts about self that you dislike?
- What are the emotions that you can sit with and tolerate? (This is when you can feel an emotion but not talk about it.)
- What are the emotions that you cannot sit with or feel intolerant towards?
- What are the emotions that you cannot verbalise?
- What are the body parts you like?
- What are the body parts that you dislike?

Write each answer in the egg and then draw a circle around each answer until the egg is full. Step back and answer the following question: Are you simple or complex? Notice that I did not say "complicated," but "complex," meaning multifaceted.

Is the answer "complex"? Good. You are a fallible human being who can and is allowed to make mistakes. If the answer is "simple," then that explains the self-damning statements you have probably been making, like "I am a failure," "I am unlovable," "I am stupid," or "I am damaged goods."

Let's not throw the baby out with the bath water; don't damn your whole self by judging your entire worth on one moment in time. A grain of sand does not make a beach, but rather a collection of grains of sands makes the beach.

Know That Unconditional Other Acceptance Is the Key

You could do the same egg exercise for someone you consider a perpetrator or even for a difficult relative and discover that, like you, that person is probably quite complex. No one individual is completely bad, just like no one is completely good. But the bitterness that can envelop us when we continue to relive an incident or a conflict can take over our lives and ruin them by making us miss out on them as we hide away with our anxiety. There is more to life than bitterness, so search for even an iota of good in everyone and learn to accept others for what they can offer. This does not mean that you need to like or love everyone you meet, but we all need to exist on this planet—some in closer proximity to us than others.

Believing That Unconditional Life Acceptance Is the Key

If your attitude is "Life absolutely should be fair and just," then expect to use up a lot of your energy trying to make it true—it's not, and living your life in a way that tries to make it true is going to be unhealthy for you. Life is not fair. It is even unjust at times. No one ever promised you anything. The world is dominated by one species—us—that is fallible and that constantly makes mistakes. Bad things do happen to good people and good things do happen to bad people. Think of a grain of sand: at times it will be exposed to sun as it forms part of a beach, and at other times it will be under the sea. We are born and die—but you have the choice of how you connect with people in all the time in between. Try right now. Talk to the person in front of you or beside you. Be authentic.

Dispassionately viewing Anxiety

Remember you are David Attenborough describing the events in your mind and compile a report into how the anxiety affects your mind and all that goes with it. Look at how it affects your thoughts, sensations and what it does to your actions. David would not make any judgements but just describe what he saw. Then being objective as possible answer the following questions:

1). Do I feel Dizzy? What are the sensations that accompany the anxiety?(Study it and describe it)

2). What am I thinking? Am I making negative predictions about the person, place, situation or future? Turning an unpleasant event into a catastrophe? Looking to control something that is outside of my control?

3). What is the anxiety telling me to do? To avoid someone, something, a situation or a place? That I must be perfect? That I have to cover up my anxiety?

Lets take a look at Chintha's story as a good example of how to use your David Attenborough skills to use when dealing with a 10 year history of anxiety.

Chintha is a 56 year old Sinhalese Sri Lankan woman who has experienced anxiety to a point of being house bound. She receives home treatment from the therapist with a view to being seen in the clinic.

Be Kind to Yourself

Let's look at some of the common self-damning statements that plague the mind of people suffering from anxiety:

- I am a failure.
- I am weird/Freak
- I need approval or else life is over
- I must be sucessful
- I am weak.
- I am pathetic.
- I am inferior.
- I am damaged goods.
- I am unlovable.
- I am boring.
- I am unlikable.

The mind can be full of negatives. When you try to overcome some of these self-damning beliefs, it can take some time to change them because you're probably in the habit of thinking in a negative vein first.

Usually global statements are used on specific occasions, like "I failed an exam, therefore I am a failure." But why do we tend to go that far? We could leave it in the moment and just say, "I failed an exam but that is life, and life goes on!" Exams can be retaken, but constant self-critical thinking can become a habit of a lifetime and a block to successful living.

The key here is to stay in the present and acknowledge it for what it is—a fleeting moment. Resist the urge to damn your whole self because of a specific instance. Would you throw out a whole car just because it had a damaged bumper? Would you destroy a whole house because of the rising damp in the bathroom? The answer to both of those questions is a resounding no! So then why set yourself unrealistic expectations of perfection?

There is no rule in the universe that states you have to be good at everything, at all times, for the rest of your life. It's OK to be unsure about yourself at times. No one expects you to be Superman or Superwoman. We each have a job to do—once you discover your unique quality, celebrate it. Celebrate being human and alive.

Let's go USA all the way! Try weaving Unconditional Self-Acceptance statements into your inner thoughts:

- I can make mistakes.
- I am allowed to make mistakes.
- I am only human.
- I am not all bad.
- I do not always fail.
- I fail sometimes.
- Life happens; I can deal with it.
- I can cope sometimes.
- I am lovable at times.
- I am not always lovable.
- I was damaged, but now I am OK.
- It's good to be me!
- I am not always weak.
- I am weak sometimes.

- ◆ I am not having a heart attack its just an anxiety symptom
- ◆ Its ok to be freakish just like so many others in the world!

These are hopeful statements, and they are all true of the human experience. We are inherently flawed. All you have to do to prove that statement is to look at the world news. As a species, we have not gotten it right yet, but one day…and herein lies the hope.

The Prejudice Model

Let's use the word "prejudice" instead of "self-damning." Let's also look at a what-if situation: If I sat down next to you and I told you I had a prejudice against black people or gay people, what would you say? You might ask me some questions about my prejudice to try and gain an understanding about my rationale for my prejudice and investigate what age it started.

When I walk onto a train full of people, what do I notice? When I walk into a pub or club, what do I notice? On both occasions, say I notice the black people or gay people first. Perhaps my attention has been highly attuned to picking them out because of some early childhood experience. I might say that my father had a big influence on my racist and homophobic ideas. Once I understand that context, I can begin to understand why I have these unhelpful thoughts—but how can I change them and how long will it take?

For some, it may take a short time and for others longer. The fact is, by acknowledging that you're having feelings, you have opened a window that gives you the opportunity to change. You just have to decide that you wish to take it.

Why have I used a racial and homophobic prejudice when discussing self-acceptance? Because the toxicity of the thought can be similar to thoughts we have about ourselves. If it is possible to change ideas that are as often-ingrained as racial and homophobic ideas to more tolerant and accepting ideas, then it should be possible to change ideas about ourselves as well.

Let's look at your self-damning beliefs and spend some time in looking at when you started to see things the way you do. When you have these thoughts, is there a pattern to when and where you have them?

Pit Stop Exercise: Spend time exploring some possible ideas about when your attention becomes highly attuned to the self-damning thoughts. In what situations do they pop up? What are the conditions?

Some psychotherapists call this process a "formulation of the problem," which is a starting place for developing some compassion from within. If you can understand how and why the thoughts affect you, then it can be reassuring to see that there is a reason for them. You have found a reasonable explanation as to why you are plagued with such thoughts.

The prejudice model is a useful way to help you see that you can judge yourself just as harshly as racists or homophobes judge others. It can also help you identify the types of situations when you begin to apply the judgment. That means you've become aware of the triggers, and now you can incorporate ideas on how to slightly change your finely tuned barometer to be more balanced in your viewpoint.

Stages of developing self-compassion:

- Understanding
- Warmth
- Flexibility
- Courage
- Empathy
- Sympathy
- Acceptance
- Forgiveness

Fig 6.2 Formulation of my Beliefs and Rules

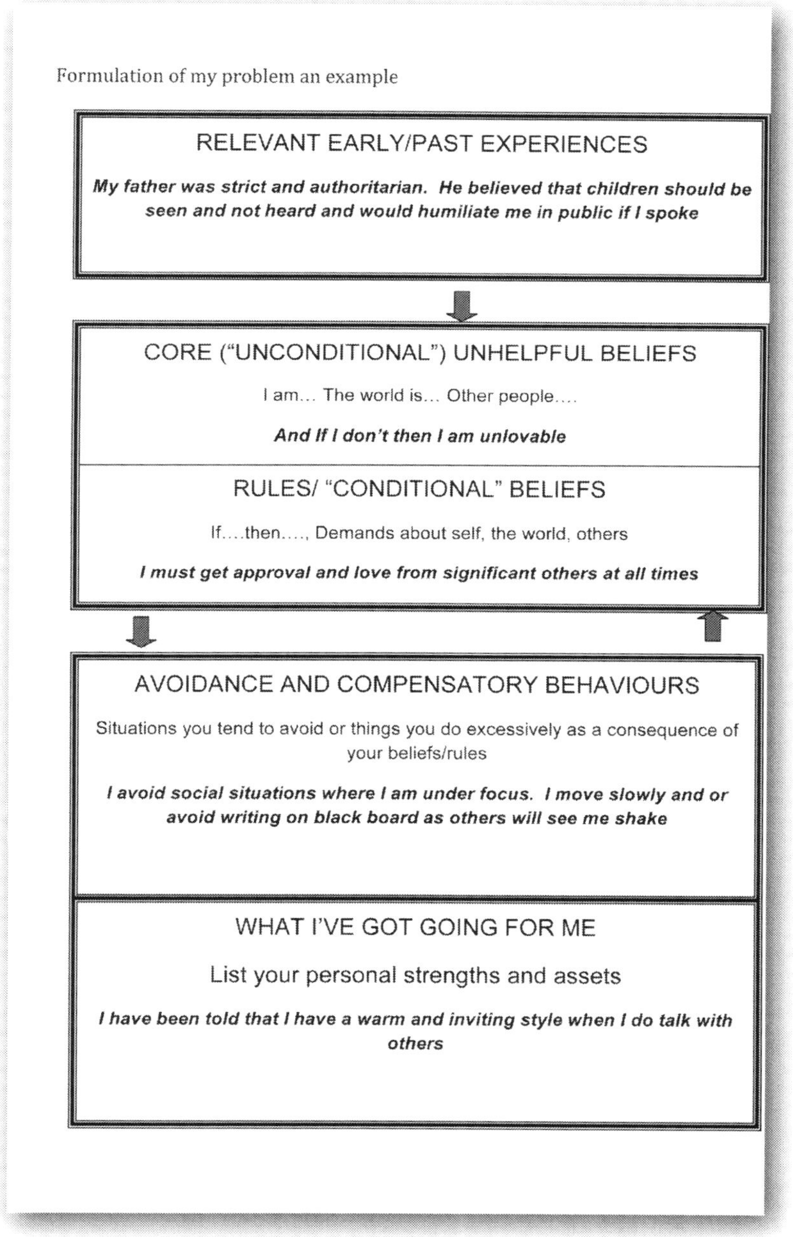

Formulation of my problem an example

RELEVANT EARLY/PAST EXPERIENCES

*My father was strict and authoritarian. He believed that children should be
seen and not heard and would humiliate me in public if I spoke*

CORE ("UNCONDITIONAL") UNHELPFUL BELIEFS

I am… The world is… Other people….

And If I don't then I am unlovable

RULES/ "CONDITIONAL" BELIEFS

If….then…., Demands about self, the world, others

I must get approval and love from significant others at all times

AVOIDANCE AND COMPENSATORY BEHAVIOURS

Situations you tend to avoid or things you do excessively as a consequence of
your beliefs/rules

*I avoid social situations where I am under focus. I move slowly and or
avoid writing on black board as others will see me shake*

WHAT I'VE GOT GOING FOR ME

List your personal strengths and assets

*I have been told that I have a warm and inviting style when I do talk with
others*

Taking One Step at a Time—and Being Content

Trying to address your self-damning thoughts with a little experimental approach and or a few new ideas is my definition of madness. Madness, to me, means repeating the same behaviours over and over and hoping for different results each time.

When we respond to self-damning thoughts, it's often with quite serious actions. The self-talk might go like this, "I cannot bear the thought of being a failure." The action in response might be to not show up for a work presentation. Changing that serious of an attitude is going to take an equally serious effort.

But what would happen if you did do something different and it impacted the self-damning thoughts? Is experiencing the thought worse than experiencing the failure itself? Experiment with experiencing the thought and see if you can bear it—tolerating the seemingly intolerable a few times in a row can be a useful muscle to build in the mind-gym workout. Go get pumping that muscle!

By taking it one step at a time, you may start to develop evidence that Theory A, which would be "I am a failure all the time," starts to be replaced by Theory B, which would be "Sometimes I fail at things, but other times I do not—this is life and it is OK to make mistakes and fail."

I hope it is Theory B that you develop a strong portfolio of evidence for; this is the helpful thought that will bring peace and help you live in the moment.

Realising That You Don't Have to Be Superhuman

The journey towards High Frustration Tolerance (HFT) is challenging but well worth it. HFT allows us to function effectively even without having "all our boxes ticked." It supports the idea that we don't have to be superman or good at everything and that we can step forward without knowing fully what will happen next.

Low Frustration Tolerance (LFT) is the opposite. When we live in a pattern of using self-damning thoughts, our mind demands to know with absolute certainty what will happen next so we can assess whether we should attempt something or avoid it altogether. The thinking pattern of LFT is that we believe we must have all the boxes ticked in order to move forward.

Understanding That It's What You Do Next That Counts

LFT tends to lead to stress. The experience is of self-talk like "I can't bear it," or "I can't bear the thought of X" quickly makes life become limiting and stagnant. The best way to test out some new behaviours aimed at improving our LFT is simply to take a risk!

It might be surprising to see that you can and do overcome your difficulties. Once you realise this, you'll race towards HFT. HFT helps us to acknowledge that we are human, and that we are fallible. We have good thoughts and bad thoughts. We all experience difficult emotions—this is part of the human experience.

If you find looking to the past depressing and looking to the future worrying, try checking in with the present moment to see what that brings—you might be surprised.

Appreciating Your Worth as a Human Being

Stepping back and looking at the bigger picture is a sure way of seeing the many aspects, both good and bad, of your personality and character. Looking at the circumstances of your own place in your family may hold some clues about why you place little value on yourself. For instance, a patient I was working with came to me one day and said "I am worthless goods." When we explored this judgment further, he told me that his elder sister had once told him in anger that "mother did not want you—she was considering an abortion!"

He remembered this because it fit into how he thinks about the world. The facts were there to support his sister's statement. His mother had not spent much time with him at all, and this led to several hours of brooding daily, a negative experience. We explored his early life and looked at it from many angles. One positive interpretation he could see that fitted well for with his other experiences was "I must be a born fighter!" When he looked back over his life, he could see much evidence to support that claim. Even in the womb, he had fought to survive! From that moment on he was less negative, more optimistic, and viewed periods of anxiety not as evidence that he must be unwell and anxious, but simply as evidence that he was alive.

Now he views negative and anxious moments as simply part of the human condition. Whereas before, he would view a problem like approval seeking as being abnormal and demand more of himself but now he acknowledges it as a normal human behaviour and does not focus too much attention on it. Changing the way he viewed one aspect of his life resulting in an ability to change how he viewed all aspects of his life and engage in life with vitality and positivity.

Being Bad Isn't the End of the World!

Parents will be very familiar with this concept. When a child wants something and the parent denies their request, the child will often lash out in disappointment and say, "I hate you! I wish I had a different father!" That sounds like a heavy blow on the surface, but we are able to acknowledge that it is generated in anger and frustration, so we quickly move on. The parent can see that this is part of a child's development—he or she is simply expressing what they think in a safe environment.

It's OK for adults to be bad sometimes, too, as long as we are able to remember who we truly are and remain certain in that knowledge. Sometimes we get caught up in the idea of looking good, for example, because we fear disapproval from others. We would do better to try out the attitude "let me try my best to look good." Healthy adults try something and then, if they fail, they try another route next time. Some people may think of you as being "bad" in the moments when you do fail, but this is a small price to pay for overall happiness and a feeling that you are achieving growth.

> *MOTTO: Don't be defined by one moment. Falling into the trap of defining your whole nature because of one experience is not useful for successful living. Accept the mistake, apologise if necessary, and move on.*

Stepping Back to Take a Good Look

The mind can get caught up in the obsession of chasing perfection. This can only lead to being angry with yourself, and if you beat yourself up constantly, you're sure to lower your mood and self-esteem.

> *Pause: Look back over times when you beat yourself up. Think what you would do if a visitor came to your house and, once you opened the door, he slapped you in the face! Would you ever open the door again? I can hear you saying "Yes, repeatedly." Well, try keeping the door closed and look for a positive twist on your situation or, if you cannot find one, then delay opening the door or even just let the doorbell ring—it won't kill you!*

The mind has many habits, like keeping hold of happy thoughts and pushing out threatening ones. Emotions may come and go like a wave, or they may flood over you. Looking at what the mind does when you experience thoughts/images and feelings is looking at the bigger picture. When you begin to develop your mindfulness practice, you will naturally be in the beginner's mind. At times you may find it difficult to stay with difficult thoughts and feelings, but as you continue you will move towards the wise mind and this will become easier. This is good news—it means the obstacles you placed in front of yourself are slowly melting away and you are beginning to realise your potential.

Finding Fault with the Concept of Self-Confidence

We are not wired to be superhuman. Look at your talents and see them as a great embellishment to being alive. As with self-esteem, the self-confidence concept risks jumping into the self-rating game, and we know now that can be perilous and can reinforce negative or unhealthy attitudes. Once you start saying "I must be able to do all these things to be complete," not being able to do them will be a recipe for disaster.

Developing Task Confidence

Let's move towards a realistic perspective. Developing task confidence will help you focus on rewarding yourself for things you *can* do. Have you ever thought about why you might be good at one thing but not another? Let's break it down. First, it's probably because of practice, practice, practice! Next, it's probably because you were able to troubleshoot to improve and make yourself better at whatever that talent is. Enjoyment follows when we recognise that we are able to do something well. And when we become good enough at something and have repeated the action enough, doing it becomes intuitive.

It's the same—but in reverse—for tasks that you are *not* good at. You probably have little or no practice at doing them. So it follows you have no experience troubleshooting that task and you haven't had a chance to develop that skill. No enjoyment follows, so you don't voluntarily return to trying that task again, instead you opt to avoid it. Often when I hear "I have no confidence at all," it's because someone isn't good at one specific thing. When they break the task down and evaluate it in small chunks, however, they are able to accomplish at least a portion of the task and consequently begin to feel a sense of achievement and well-being.

Phase Three

PENULTIMATE PART OF THE JOURNEY:
MOVING ON AND MAINTAINING GAINS

CHAPTER 7

Techniques for Changing and Moving Forward

In This Chapter You Will

- ◆ Learn to move from the beginner mind into the wise mind
- ◆ Accept that saying no is OK sometimes
- ◆ Learn meditating exercises to get you started

This chapter is about putting the talk into walking, or practicing some new ideas and evaluating the results. I often liken therapy to clothes shopping—you try on a garment to see if it fits and if it does, then you buy it and wear it all the time. If you don't like it in the store, however, then you won't like it at home. This chapter gives you the opportunity to try out some techniques and to see if they benefit you. Remember: taking the risk of consciously trying to change your behaviour is courageous as you don't know what to expect. All I would ask of you now is that you expect *something* to happen. In this chapter, I show you some key techniques for how to living mindfully each day, whilst also revealing at some tips for being assertive and proactive. Being mindful does not mean passively accepting things that happen to you. It means finding a process that helps you develop into the person you want to be.

Living Mindfully Day to Day

We are all tempted by habit to fill the mind with endless lists of all the things that need doing. These can be tasks and chores, but also unhelpful stuff. Stuff like worrying about all the things you need to spend money on when clearly there is some in the bank, or worrying about how your child will act when he turns eighteen even though he is still only four years old! We need to train our minds to archive certain concerns until later. As you proceed through your day, ask yourself at several points whether your mind is filling up with unnecessary concerns.

Pit Stop Exercise: Use your five senses to look, hear, taste, touch, and smell your surroundings as though you were a tourist who had just arrived in a foreign country. Evaluate what is around you as if the environment is brand-new to you. By generating even an artificial newfound curiosity for your surroundings, you will postpone thinking negative or "filler" thoughts for a while. This will also give you a break from the usual mental habits of brooding and worrying. It will allow you to "just be" in the moment for a few minutes.

Discovering the New, Healthy You

What are you like when your usual over activity slows down? Do you like you? Do you not know because you've never tried it? When you slow things down, you give yourself the chance to get to know the real you! The one who is able to sit, listen, and take action in a meaningful way.

Often when life gets too busy, our minds buzz with all sorts of junk. Meditation gives us a reason to stop and take a look at just one piece of your life or the life around you. Meditating can be frustrating at first, because the beginner mind is trained to fill up with the obstacles such as statements of "I cannot do this," "this is boring," or "I can't bear to just sit here in silence." Stay with it, however—you'll quickly get past these obstacles and then begin to discover the new, healthy you.

The new you will be able to sit with good, neutral, and bad thoughts, feelings, and sensations. You will not be emotionally impacted by these thoughts and feelings, instead you'll be able to learn from them, and to learn that lead to new learning.

Detective Columbo, Please Sign Up for Duty!

The mind is prone to negativity. That fact is particularly unhelpful to people suffering from anxiety! The mind is built with a fight-or-flight mechanism, which is the brain's way of trying to keep you safe. As babies, we are born with the amygdala intact—this section of the brain processes emotions like anxiety, disgust, anger, low mood, and joy.

The mind is wired for emotions. The amygdala's job is to keep the baby safe by teaching it to interpret different emotional experiences, so it acts like a pattern-recognition program. For instance, when you smile down at your baby and express joy, the baby will look up and smile back— that "programs" the baby to experience joy. This is the first experience of communication. Images like that aid in the process of bonding and attachment—it helps the baby feel safe.

Anxiety is interpreted in a similar way. When you are confronted with a feared object or situation, you are programmed with an instinct to either run or to fight it. Either approach will lead to a neutralizing of the anxiety in the end. You'll feel safe once you've either run away from the threat or beaten it down, and that completes the pattern. This can cause problems in terms of emotional threats, however, because the mind will remember which behaviours kept you safe and will suggest repeating them when confronted with a similar threat in the future. This can make an emotional problem worse.

You need to be like Detective Columbo and learn to detect safety-seeking behaviours so you can arrest them. Standing in the corner to avoid social contact because you fear it, but later walking away and feeling alone or feeling certain that everyone must hate you because no one talked to you is an example. Challenge yourself to try standing in the middle of a group; say the first thing that pops into your head. If people begin to talk with you, then you'll learn that the negative thoughts don't hold any truth.

By being a detective on the lookout for "criminal" thoughts about yourself, you will learn to search for alternatives to the many negative thoughts that plague the mind. Just like Columbo, be curious. Revisit the scenes of earlier "crimes" to find clues about what caused the crime in the first place. There is always more than one way to view a problem if you put in the work to find it.

Learning to Be Off Duty

Obsessive thoughts and images, by definition, come at us 24/7!! Let's use A&E departments as an example of how to cope with intense experiences and thoughts. When nurses or doctors are working, they cannot be on duty 24/7 or else they will exhaust themselves, have a breakdown, or even kill someone because they might not be able to complete a critical treatment with care and attention. They are likely to be irritable and not make the best decisions. Since we always have thoughts, it's difficult not to constantly be on duty. But the irritability caused by that situation that will inevitably creep in is going to mar your decision-making process.

To stop accidents from happening, doctors and nurses are simply not allowed to work more than a certain number of hours per day. They also have a rota—that safeguards them and the patients rolling through. In some cases, doctors must be told to leave. They often get so involved with caring for a crash victim that they don't realise they have stayed way past the end of their shift. If it's good for doctors and nurses to be forced to have off-duty time, it must be good for you, too, right? Try deferring judgment on a thought you're having right now until later. You may wish to return to it later—that's OK, because you will have left some space between the trigger and the reaction. When you learn to delay responding to thoughts and feelings, eventually they will stop plaguing you 24/7.

Rediscovering Relationships

Relationships are often the first casualty of anxiety. Friends and family often do not know how to react to someone with anxiety or what to do to help you. Including them in your life is a necessary and important step to managing and overcoming its grips.

You'll be surprised how readily people who care about you will be willing to forgive you for having withdrawn yourself. Start by saying "Hello. Sorry I have been out of contact, but…" This is a good way to break the ice with people who have not seen you for a while. Use technology to help you if the idea of an intense initial conversation is overwhelming: text or get in touch again via social media first. They can be useful for making tentative steps towards re-entering society.

Anxiety holds you captive like a dictator. But guess what? Mindfulness can help you create a democracy in your mind anytime. Break the silence by choosing to live for today and tell people that you are interested in being included in activities.

If you are unsure of what to do about your anxiety, then surely those observing it are equally unsure and confused. As you get to know yourself—and to know yourself with the illness—then you have already won the biggest battle.

Fig 7.1 Your Bill of Rights

Top tip: Bill of Rights
Generate a list of statements to motivate you in your journey:

I have the right to be an anxiety-free father.
I have the right to a anxiety-free life!
I have the right to be an anxiety-free husband.

By having these affirmations at hand, they can bring about a positive motivation to keep going with your mindfulness treatment. Get militant and be fired up about blasting anxiety out of your life.

Learning to Say No

Anxiety is sometimes called "the yes illness." That's because many who experience it are often people pleasers or approval seekers. Our days are filled with many things to do, which can leave us feeling overwhelmed, especially if we believe we have failed to please everyone.

Learning to say no is about understanding the simple truth that you are turning down a request, not a person. It may feel bad to say no to someone. It may even seem intolerable to disappoint someone else, but the truth is that it becomes tolerable after you do it a few times.

Saying no is important for your own self-preservation. It can save a lot of energy so you have it to spend on things and people that are important to you. Not being able to say no often means that you end up spending time with things and people you do *not* want to spend or dedicate time to, and you will resent yourself for not saving your energy for things or people you care about.

Fig 7.2 The Broken-Record Technique

Pit Stop Exercise: The Broken Record Technique.
You can teach yourself to say no over and over, and to learn that when you do, you don't need to give an explanation. This is an important skill to have mastered so that when someone plays to your emotions or sense of guilt with a request, you can stand firm. For example, if someone asks you to babysit and says that they need you to or else they won't be able to do their work, you have to realise that finding childcare is their problem, not yours. Say no and keep repeating it until they get the message. You may worry that the person will perceive you as being difficult, but with practice you'll learn that supporting someone doesn't mean giving into his or her every request. Saying no will help you to focus on your own priorities.

Another reason may well be an Idea for Living on intimacy or mental health. When looking at Ideas or philosophies for living use two questions to develop one. Q1: How do I want to be remembered? Q2: How would I like others to remember me?

Fig 7.3 The Cross Roads Model

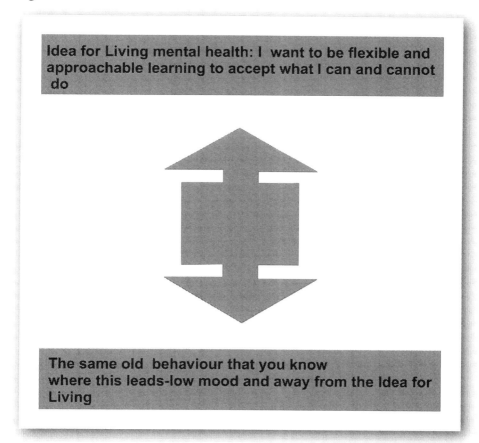

Idea for Living mental health: I want to be flexible and approachable learning to accept what I can and cannot do

The same old behaviour that you know where this leads-low mood and away from the Idea for Living

The Crossroad Model

Imagine yourself at a crossroad. You are presented with a choice of direction. You can either engage in the same old, self-defeating behaviours that you know will move you away from one of your Ideas for Living or you can choose to engage in an alternative behaviour that may give you a sense of moving towards an Idea for Living. Just think of one behaviour—it will act like a domino effect and lead to others. To help further, you may want to do your own analysis using TRAP which is an acronym for Trigger, Response And Problem. And TRAC is Trigger, Response and Coping strategy.

Situation: A colleague asks you if you would like to go to lunch. Unfortunately, you cannot go. The colleague takes this as a rejection.

Question: What to grab some lunch?

Trigger: Sorry, I can't. I need to continue working.

Response: Colleague feels foolish and anxious.

And problem: Colleague returns to desk and broods

You can see that this is TRAPping away from the colleague's Idea for Living: Being a light, bright, and cheerful worker, able to take things in stride and not be shaken easily.

Let's look at the same situation but using the TRAC towards the Idea for Living.

Trigger: Sorry, I can't. I need to continue working.

Response: Colleague feels foolish and anxious.

And Coping: Colleague simply asks someone else.

Allowing Yourself to Be Happy

This is often a major obstacle in recovery. Attitudes such as "I don't deserve to be happy" or "I must be happy at all times" have a detrimental effect on wellness. This attitude is most often linked to shame.

> *MOTTO: If you don't deal first with the shame, then you won't be able to unlock the door! What this means is that by disclosing the shameful secret you can then move forward to explore your journey to happiness. Many are in therapy for years talking about other things not relevant trying to avoid the shameful secret Work on it and blast the closet doors open, as it will be worth it!*

If you struggle to sit calmly with positive thoughts and emotions, try a gradual exercise of sitting with one until you get to a point of achievement. The point of achievement is relative to you and your situation. Then use a critical thought to stop the experience. Build up on the length of time you spend sitting calmly on each subsequent occasion—and remember as you do that you are working to reclaim your life from anxiety!

Defining Yourself by Your Present

If you make a mistake, welcome to the club! Membership is open to all! It does you and others no favour to blame yourself for making one mistake. All humans make mistakes—and often repeat the same mistake. We are wired to be imperfect. It is wonderfully liberating to live life with this knowledge that we can all have moments of being foolish, socially inarticulate, boring, crazy, an idiot, happy, fucked up, misguided etc

Getting Out of Your Comfort Zone

Trying something new is always a good idea. It blows away the cobwebs in our mind and brings about some creative thinking and feelings. Anxiety, as we've noted, is a process of life-shrinkage. Slowly but surely you begin cutting people, activities, and ideas out of your life. It may start with mild anxiety, but it quickly creeps up on you; soon you find yourself responding with experiential avoidance. Quickly, you're left with only negative thoughts about loss, punishment, and self-criticism.

Often when you feel your life has shrunk, the only way out is to push it back into its former dimension. Start by taking up the roles and activities you enjoyed previously, then encourage yourself to grow it out past the boundaries of where it was before, with a twist. The twist is to face some of the blind spots that you usually try to avoid. Many clients have benefitted from facing their nemeses, whether that be a mountain-load of bills, decluttering a house full of hoarded stuff, or changing the dynamic of a relationship, to name a few.

Psychobabble Defined: Madness is doing something over and over again, expecting different results.

———•———

Pit Stop Exercise: Try adding a twist to your weekly routine and face your avoidances today. Then rate your mood before and after the activity. Does your mood improve?

———•———

Fig 7.4 Practice exercises in meditation

Mindfulness Meditations

Body-Scan Meditation: Sit or lie down in a comfortable position. Take a minute or two to breathe deeply and relax. Close your eyes and bring your focus to the present moment and your physical self. This is a physically passive technique, so you do not need to move, flex, or do anything else with your body. There is, however, nothing wrong with moving a part of your body if you feel that it would be helpful to work out any "kinks." Begin the body scan by drawing your attention to one particular part of your body. Try starting with your feet. Tune in to what is happening with your feet. What do you notice? Do your best to remain as passive and nonjudgmental as possible. (Remember: you are acting as an objective observer of your own subjective experience.) At the same time, carefully observe your feet. Try to feel both deep inside them and on the surface. If you notice tension, tightness, or contracted muscles, consciously release and relax those areas.

When you feel ready, progress up to your lower legs. Again, notice what is happening in them. Carefully observe how they feel from both deep inside them and on the surface. If you notice tension, tightness, or contracted muscles, consciously release and relax those areas. Progress now to the upper half of your legs and repeat the exercise. From there, move on to your buttocks, waist, and lower abdomen. Next, focus on your middle abdomen, sides, and back. Your chest and upper back are up next, followed by your shoulders, upper and lower arms, and then hands. Once you have finished focusing on your hands and fingers, move your attention to your neck. Finally, turn your focus to your face, jaw, eyes, ears, and skull.

Finish this exercise by taking a few more deep breaths and turning your awareness back to your entire physical self, which includes all of the parts on which you have been focusing.

For a quicker body scan, try focusing on larger sections of your body at a time (for example, focus on your full legs as one section). For a more in-depth body scan, try focusing on smaller sections of your body (for example, each finger or even each toe). A very quick body scan can take just thirty seconds. A longer body scan can take thirty minutes—or more. Based on your needs and circumstances, this exercise can be very flexible.

Breathing into the Tension: When you feel tension somewhere, then develop curiosity as to why it has come about, i.e. do you exhale in distress or do you hold your breath? Or something else? Then perform the opposite action from what you believe has caused the tension initially. Breathe if know you tend to hold your breath, and so on.

Sitting with the Breath: When sitting or lying down, focus on the belly as you breathe. Keep your back straight. Do this simple action for ten minutes daily. Each time the mind wanders, note where it went but then bring it gently back to your belly. Remember: your mind will wander a thousand times—it's your job to bring in back to the belly after each thought. Be kind to yourself and congratulate yourself on having made the effort to meditate in the first place.

Doing Bath-Time Exercises: This is useful for clients who self-harm when experiencing distress. It might help you try to resist the urge to cut yourself, for example. Draw water and feel it run over your hand as it pours into the bath. Add bubble bath solution and smell the fragrance. Feel the bubbles in your hand. Smear some bubbles on your face just for the sensation of it and watch how the steam gradually fogs up the mirror. Use your senses to tap fully into the simple experience of treating yourself to a pampering bath.

Practicing the Opposite-Action Exercise: This exercise is simply about trying an opposite action to what you always do so you can test out the results. For example, if you always say no to going out with friends lately, then try saying yes sometimes. Evaluate how you feel afterwards. If you are stubborn about a certain issue, then try consciously to be more flexible. And so on—this can apply to many different situations.

CHAPTER 8

Taking Your Next Steps and Going Beyond

In This Chapter You Will

- Familiarise yourself with which professionals can help you to get better
- Look at the whole you and learn how to improve your physical health
- Make the most of your awareness skills as you march towards wellness

You're doing well with the mindfulness-based CBT practice, but now you need other information to help you go further. What's next? Learning to talk with doctors and learning how to make sense of medications. Trying to interface with medical professionals can be a headache to say the least, but I hope I smooth the path ahead for you a little. There are many services available—both in the NHS and the private sector. You're in the driver's seat, so do yourself a favor and link mental health services with physical care teams. Take charge of your own health. In this chapter, I will cover how some common long-term conditions can affect depression as well as the big topic of taking a holistic approach to health and providing yourself with a seamless service for your own recovery.

Meeting Doctors, Patients, and People

There are many mental health professionals out there, and admittedly their titles can all kind of sound the same. Knowing with whom you are talking with is key to knowing what to ask for.

Psychiatrists: These are medically trained doctors who know about the physical body and how it affects the mind. They will assess you to look for physical problems that could be leading to a mental health problem. For example, they may perform blood tests to check out thyroid activity. If you suffer form hypothyroidism, then it could indicate depressive symptoms; if you suffer from hyperthyroidism, it may contribute to anxiety symptoms. They also use the Mental Health Act powers and commonly listed as the "Responsible Person in Care" in any legal documents that may be related to detainment. They have the power to admit a patient to hospital if they deem that person to be a danger to him or herself or to others.

General Practitioners: These are medically trained doctors who have experience treating many different ailments; in training, they are expected to rotate through a lot on different placements in departments like men's health, stomach problems, brain and head injuries, etc. They have broad medical knowledge about lots of things, but they are not specialists. However, they will refer you to a specialist team if they suspect that would be the best course of treatment for you.

Psychologists: They have an undergraduate degree in psychology and are aware of broad aspects of the science of psychology. They may advance their training by taking additional courses in CBT, Gestalt Therapy, Psychodynamic Therapy, etc., which they then use to treat patients according to which approach they think will most benefit the patient.

Clinical Psychologists: They will have completed a degree in psychology and then proceeded with further training to become a doctor of clinical psychology. They treat patients, develop services, and can hold Mental Health Section powers by being listed as a Responsible Person in Care. They can detain you in hospital if you are a danger to yourself or others.

Psychotherapists: These are drawn from many health-care backgrounds like nursing, occupational therapy, and social work. They will have master's degree–level training in a therapy approach like CBT, Gestalt, etc.

Some continue training and achieve a doctoral status through research into a patient problems like anxiety, etc.

Counselling Psychologists: They will have completed a degree in psychology and then proceeded with further training at the doctoral level. They treat patients and develop services.

Health Psychologists: These will have completed a degree in psychology and then proceeded with further training at the doctoral level. They treat patients and develop services for long-term conditions like asthma, diabetes, stroke, heart problems, multiple sclerosis, etc. that are often found to cause mental health issues like depression. They also look into health-care policies to try and further the understanding of what causes our habits and can act as advisors to government.

Counsellors: These can be from any background and may have attended training as short as a two-day course or as long as a six-month course. They can legally call themselves counsellors after having received any amount of certified training. Note that the term counsellor is often used interchangeably with psychotherapist, so it is worth investigating whether they have the same level of training as a psychotherapist before enlisting their services. Many will show their experience and training on LinkedIn or on their own websites, and you should also be able to cross-check it on accreditation societies' sites.

> *Top Tip: Remember that health care professionals are ordinary people. It is important that you feel comfortable with the one you think you would like to continue seeing for a duration of time. Make sure you feel that he or she understands you and your problem. If you don't feel comfortable with someone for any reason—perhaps he is not sociable or simply does not seem to understand you very well—them move on and find another. You should avoid any mental health professional who becomes defensive when asked about the training he or she received.*

The therapeutic process is guaranteed to be an emotional journey, and that's going to be difficult enough. Don't exacerbate how hard it is for you by staying with a doctor or counsellor who doesn't seem able to connect with you. Shop around.

Therapy is like going clothes shopping. A good therapist should allow you to try out some different techniques in sessions to see if they fit. Once you try one out and it works, then you will feel more trusting of the therapy processes and be able to make gains to achieve your goal.

Cluing into Long-Term Conditions and Their Impacts on Depression

Many of us suffer from a long-term condition like asthma, diabetes, stroke, heart problems, etc. It used to be that health services would be split in two camps: one service for physical problems and the other for mental problems. Now the government is looking to change this by joining services together, which will provide a virtually seamless therapy to the patient.

This step in the right direction, but how well this currently translates into the services structure is another thing entirely. It's estimated that £30 million minimum per year is lost to cancelled appointments and surgeries due to mental illness. This begs the question of whether the government's infrastructure is up to the challenge of integrating the two fields of care. There is a need to pull in the private sector, which can provide bespoke care as a compliment to or as an alternative to NHS treatments.

Dealing with Diabetes

It is routine now for GPs to carry out a mini-assessment on diabetics to check for problems like anxiety and depression. If a patient does not pass the review, they are referred to mental health services in the NHS. The waiting list for services can fluctuate in length. Early stages of diabetes are the most tricky period to treat—many live in denial and refuse to make changes to their lifestyle even faced with a diagnosis. Early detection is not a problem, but early treatment is. Promising research has shown that those newly diagnosed may be able to reverse some of the effects of diabetes if they follow a strictly controlled program for the first six months. The medical community has reached no firm conclusions about whether this is categorically true, but it is worth investigating if you want to know more.

There are two types of diabetes:

Type 1 develops when the insulin-producing cells in the body have been destroyed, therefore making it difficult for the body to produce insulin. Insulin is like the key to the door of each cell; it manages the amount of glucose allowed into the cell. Glucose build up outside the door can cause many different problems.

Type 2 develops when the insulin-producing cells in the body are unable to produce enough insulin or when the insulin that is produced is not working properly.

Surveying Strokes

Strokes are the third-biggest killer for women in the UK, but many of us do not even know the warning signs that one may be on the way or occurring. Blood pressure provides the first clue; if high, the first treatment is to change your lifestyle to bring it under control or back within healthy limits. A "funny turn" is another warning sign. This is when you seem disconnected from reality for a moment. Specialists call these Transient Ischemic Attacks (TIAs). These are really mini-strokes and need to be treated. CBT is often very effective for those who have had a stroke and have been left severely impaired initially but with therapy have regained the function of their arms, legs and life skills again. Once discharged from neurologists, many stroke victims go on to suffer anxiety and may need talking therapies to help.

Top Tip: F.A.S.T
F Facial weakness: Can the person smile? Has their face fallen on one side?

A Arm weakness: Can the person raise both arms and keep them there?

S Speech problems: Can the person speak clearly and understand what you say? Is their speech slurred?

T Time: If you see any one of these three signs, it's TIME to call 999. Stroke is always a medical emergency that requires immediate medical attention.

Having Knowledge of Heart Problems

The science behind the studies about happiness show that being happy leads to success; that is, success does not lead to happiness. The UK now is a wealthy country, but its general population rates low in overall happiness. Feelings of happiness can lead in up to a 10 percent reduction in blood pressure and heart events. High blood pressure is one of the biggest causes of a stroke or heart failure. Stressful lifestyles *will* cause high blood pressure, so it is important to look at factors that develop happiness to create equilibrium. Rational Emotive Behaviour Therapy research into rigid, demanding thinking styles highlighted a strong link to high blood pressure. When participants changed to flexible thinking styles, a significant reduction in blood pressure levels took place. Lets apply flexible thinking during this period of economic uncertainty and not let it have an impact on the heart, let's see how creative you can be when limitations imposed on you by having less money are placed upon you. At such times, creativity is the best remedy!

Being Aware of Bodily Distress

Bodily Distress is a condition that used to be known as a "musculoskeletal condition" (MSK) and was lumped under the umbrella of medically unexplained conditions. Now, however, experts are changing the name to Bodily Distress; many believe this to be a better label. Research continues to address the cause of the pain sufferers of this condition experience. Mindfulness-Based Stress Reduction (MBSR) has proven to be effective in reducing this type of pain. Let me qualify that by saying that I don't think that the *causes* of the pain disappear after MBSR, but factors causing the pain, like stress, are reduced and so may ameliorate overall pain levels and help increase functioning. Bodily Distress is a serious condition that significantly reduces quality of life, but therapy approaches MBCT, CBT and REBT can help to improve that quality.

Comprehending Cancer

A diagnosis of cancer is no longer as final as it once was just fifteen or twenty years ago. Many in recovery and remission learn to live life fully again. But, understandably, when many first receive the diagnosis, they live in denial and find it difficult to come to terms with the news. This can delay treatment. Therapy can aid in getting treatment underway by helping patients face their fears.

The percentage of men who get routine screenings men is still low; they underestimate the importance of early detection. Many who do attend the screening appointments tend to view it as being a MOT, which does sound more positive than a cancer screening. We think nothing of taking the car for its annual checks, so why do we feel differently about our bodies? If you have not had a MOT, go and book an appointment with your GP today.

Understanding Multiple Sclerosis

In multiple sclerosis, the body attacks its own myelin sheath, the substance that protects nerve fibres in the brain and spinal cord. It damages the communication lines between the brain and the arms and legs, making movement more difficult as the illness progresses. A high level of stress is known to increase the disease's progression and to contribute to the patient's rate of decline. For many cases, using mindfulness and CBT to reduce stress can help slow down the progression of the illness, thus enhancing quality of life.

Moving towards a United Perspective on Health

A holistic approach to health is ideal, but in reality our access to care is limited by the structure of the healthcare business. It is easier to find a therapist to help treat both a long-term condition and a mental illness at the same time in the private sector than it is within the NHS. The NHS will refer you to two different practitioners, which means double the amount of appointments, and suddenly you can find yourself with a difficult diary to juggle.

The NHS is moving forward on this. They have learned from the private sector that it is useful and beneficial for patients to have, for instance, a CBT therapist in a physiotherapy department who can suggest a treatment plan for pain management. Taking the time to see that physical ailments are not separate from mental health is all-important. Mindfulness-Based

Cognitive Therapy has been proven to help with pain management, anxiety disorders, and depression.

Looking at Mind and Body

Many scientists have now found evidence that MBCT has a huge impact on distress. It can also change our outlook from pessimistic to optimistic through just six weeks of mindfulness practice. Mindfulness helps you to view problems from a calm remove, so instead of using demanding thinking to take away pain or stress, mindfulness will help you observe it and develop a wise mind about how to deal with it. It helps us develop understanding as to the why behind our emotions; once you have an answer or accept that the why may remain unanswered, there can be a sense of moving forward. It allows you to consider more options than you probably knew were available to you before beginnings mindfulness practice.

Working with Physical Pain

Our usual approach to pain can be a hindrance to healing. Rigid attitudes like "I must not have this pain, and the fact I do means my life is over" can actually produce more mental anguish—more pain. Understanding attitudes is an important part of self-discovery when battling with long-term conditions. A big problem in understanding pain is the cultural pressure for us to say "It's all in my head!" This is meant to help by teaching us to be stoic, but it actually does not. There are negative connotations associated with that statement and the stigma of receiving mental health treatment.

That statement is, ironically, true in the literal sense. All the things that we experience pass through our nerve centre—the brain. The brain processes everything we feel. Here is the organ we should be focusing a holistic approach on in order to make a real change. Let's get biological: without the brain, we would not feel anything or know anything. It follows, therefore, that psychology can help you with physical pain. Seeing a psychologist does not mean you're going nutty and it also does not mean that your pain must define you. Pain is part of the human experience, which unfortunately is very challenging and sometimes overwhelming. There is so much more to you than your past—you have your present and a future full of surprises.

Getting Familiar with Attitudes That Can Harm and Heal

Looking at the language we use and the intentions linked to certain words can reveal much about how we approach life. For instance, "I must" may be said in a flexible, meaningful way on occasion but on other occasions it's said with rigid inflexibility. The latter can bring about a feeling like anxiety or distress. Looking at your mind and how you interpret situations or negative thoughts by adopting this rigid stance will help you see and experiment with them. Can you see the impact of the rigid attitudes and how they create self-defeating behaviours? By having understanding on these attitudes will 50 percent of the battle already won and now the other 50 percent is about using the Mindfulness practice to make changes.

———————

Fig 8.1 Rational Emotive Imagery

> *Pit Stop Exercise: Rational Emotive Imagery*
> *With eyes closed, focus on a situation that you are troubled about and focus on the difficult emotions it brings. Spend time to ask yourself the following:*
> *What am I thinking?*
> *What style of thinking is it?*
> *Is it demanding? Negative? Self/other/life damning? I-can't-bear-it-itis?*
> *Then focus on the thinking and keep on demanding, damning, etc. until the emotion gets as bad as it can get for you. Then replace the thinking with a flexible attitude that's positive and self-appreciating—"I CAN bear it" thinking—and then watch the feeling and see it change. Describe how you feel now.*

———————

Going the Way of Awareness

Being able to notice and describe without jumping to conclusions or judgments is useful. It is also free and always an available option. Use the senses of sight, hearing, taste, touch, and smell to inform your experience and awaken your passion for life. Before you can achieve this enlightened view of your own behaviours, however, you need to train yourself not to repeat the damaging among them.

Diagnosis Corner: The definition of madness is doing the same behaviours over and over but expecting different results!

Take a risk and do something different! If you are a perfectionist in everything you do, try to leave something imperfect every day for a week. Record your results and emotions about this on a sheet of paper. If wearing perfectly coordinated outfits is one thing that keeps you from feeling stressed, for example, try mismatching. This will help you develop High Frustration Tolerance for stress.

Making the Most of New Beginnings

Whatever your life story has been up to today, it can change starting now. Everyone deserves a new start, whether you are the victim or the perpetrator of an emotional crime, change can take place. But it's up to you to do bring change to your own life—no one can force you to change. Therapists can *help* you bring change into your own life, but cannot do it all for you. Good therapists will also not allow you to become merely "seat warmers" in their office: they will continue to challenge you to grow. If motivation is low, then a therapist can help you improve it through what we call motivational work. Motivational work/interviewing is a technique that aids the growth of motivation. Motivational interviewing is non-judgmental, non-confrontational and non-directive.[6] The approach attempts to increase the client's awareness of the potential problems caused, consequences experienced, and risks faced as a result of the behavior targeted in therapy. Therapists help clients envision a better future, and become increasingly motivated to achieve it

Keeping Up with Mindfulness Practice

Moving from the beginner mind to the wise mind takes times and discipline. Just eight weeks of daily practice, however, will show a transition.

You can do anything for eight weeks, right? Research shows that conditional self-acceptance can change to more unconditional acceptance and you can begin to show evidence of self-creating compassion in just that time span, which is great news!

Role Stress

When we fuse the descriptions of ourselves with our true selves, for instance, "I am the breadwinner in the family." That may be factually true, but believing that you are your role in a family, at work, or in society can be damaging. Thought Action Fusion is trying to make something true by thinking it is true. This type of thinking forms a part many problems, such as Obsessive-Compulsive Disorder, but it also can increase stress levels.

Let's take a look at the conviction "I am strong." If you attach a lot of meaning to this belief, then you may have fused with it. This could prove problematic when others offer you help—the very thought of being "weak" enough to need any sort of help is intolerable, therefore you will reject the person offering and you may damage your relationship with that person in the process. On the flip side, if you believe that you are weak, then you will have difficulty accepting that you *can* do something well. Thinking you are weak becomes a self-fulfilling prophecy that leads to helplessness.

Try to distance yourself from the descriptions of your traits. Try writing down as many descriptions of yourself as you can, listing them in positive, negative, and neutral columns. See how many there are, but don't be surprised to see some contradictions. You may be weak in some areas but strong in others. When you look at the list now, does it make sense to rate yourself according to just one, or to single just one trait out of the dozens that you see? Not really! Learn to stop rating yourself and try to accept that you are a multifaceted—and fallible—human being.

People Stress

People do not cause stress—our perception of a situation that involves other people causes stress. We have to take responsibility of our own interpretations, and to accept that they may be wrong. After all, we humans are known to make mistakes! The interactions within us, with ourselves, with others, and with the world are many and varied. Mindfulness practice is particularly useful at reducing the "people stress."

Our internal interactions can involve the fight-or-flight mechanism designed for the job of keeping us safe, but our interpretation of safety and threat may be in question or there may be a slight possibility for an overreaction, which in turn could cause more pain and stress. Some interpretations may be unconscious at the time they happen and so may not change some of our outward reactions. Hindsight is golden, and we can develop awareness to respond to them in more useful ways in the future.

> *Diagnosis Corner: Anxiety and anger developed as responses to a perceived threat. They are governed by a small part of the brain called the amygdala. We are born with a fully formed amygdala, and its job is to protect us and keep us safe. The hippocampus processes 3-D items and gives them context, applies rational thought to what we see, where we are, and who we are with, etc. It is not fully formed when we are born, but finishes forming at approximately age four. Be kind to yourself—you are wired first to react instinctively instead of rationally.*

Work Stress

We know from many studies on both men and women that how much control we have over our situation affects our health drastically. Studies on men and heart problems show a strong correlation between jobs with low levels of personal control and a high incidence of heart conditions. Men who have jobs with high levels of personal control show a low incidence of heart conditions. Today, there are many options available that can help increase a sense of control, such as zero-hour contracts, self-employment, job-sharing, etc. Many people swear by the benefits of self-employment since it allows for more creativity than most corporate-type jobs. If you are thinking of becoming self-employed, know that there is plenty of advice online. Try reducing your paid job by one day weekly to test out you business idea to see if it is successful. If you prefer to work for a company and be someone else's employee but still associate your work environment with stress, check to see whether it might be possible to introduce some amount of flexibility or control to your job.

Food Stress

Food is close to everyone's heart, for varied reasons. So much research proves the link between eating a nutritious, balanced, and varied diet and good health. But changing poor eating habits can be difficult, and the effort comes with emotional, social, and cultural repercussions. Let me help you focus mindfully on how to change your eating habits. Have you ever focused on slowing down the way you eat, really taking time to appreciate the sensations developed on your tongue at the time you take a bite and chew?

Pit Stop Exercise: Take a raisin and roll it between your finger and thumb. Smell it and describe the smell. Feel it and describe the texture. When do you notice the saliva building up in your mouth in anticipation of eating it? Is the raisin associated with any memories that might be popping up now, in the present moment? Maybe you have a memory of your grandma baking scones and you remember their smell. Take a tiny bite and roll it around on your tongue. Describe the taste—is it bitter at times and sweet at other times? By slowing down like this, you will gain a different perspective on food that leads to a positive attitude about it.

World Stress

You might believe that the world is unfair but think it should be fair. New forms of social media and technology make it all but impossible to shut ourselves off from the 24/7 news cycle that has become the norm. We see reports of crimes as soon as they happen, and we worry about what our children are likely to see online. These make it very hard to manage stress, but if we worry that everything we read about could happen to us, then we would never leave the house!

There is no simple answer about how to combat all the kinds of stress the world can introduce, but I want to offer you the ability to step back and look at the bigger picture. When you demand that life should be fair at all times, to all people, doesn't that add pressure and a heaviness to our minds, reducing our happiness? I would prefer to have you lean towards a flexible way of thinking, like "I prefer that the world be fair at all times—but if it can't be, then I can manage in this fallen, imperfect world. Life goes on!" Developing flexibility is going to help you with reaching and attaining goals. It also will help you to be happy—and if you're happy then success may follow more readily.

Negative life experiences cause some to look at themselves as having low self-worth, but rating ourselves based on those experiences is inherently a biased proposition. There is a tendency when feeling negative emotions and thinking negative thoughts to throw everything about you into the same mental pot: "I am a failure and everything is shit!" Try to move away by not fusing such thoughts with your idea of self. Thought Action Fusion is a term psychotherapists use, which is also known as "magical thinking." In lay terms, it translates to "I think it, therefore it will come true."

A description of the world like "the world is against me" sounds good when you say it at a cocktail party, but it is problematic if you fuse with it and associate it strongly with your total identity. It may lead to you not accept any alternative views or to treat others as bad influences as well, leading to alienation. Try not to be defined by one moment, action, or episode of your life. Instead, join all the descriptions together into one drawing like the egg exercise in Chapter 6 suggests in order to see how complex life really is.

CHAPTER 9

Reducing Your Chance of Relapse

In This Chapter You Will

- ♦ Learn why backing up is always a key to wellness
- ♦ Fine-tune your toolkit for long living
- ♦ Impress upon yourself that practice, practice, practice makes permanent!

As you come to the end of your journey with anxiety, it's important to reflect back on all the progress you've made and to consolidate your work in order to make the changes permanent. Remember: practice makes permanent! Many drop out of therapy at the stage when they begin to feel better. They feel ready to move on and believe that their struggles are all behind them. But the end stage is just as important as the assessment and treatment phases. Take the time to remember, appreciate, and participate in the tending of the garden that is the mind. Gardeners will understand that time, tenderness, and knowledge are all needed to make a garden thrive. An overgrown garden filled with weeds will take longer and be more difficult to clean up. Tender, loving care is needed for the mind, too. Don't let it get overgrown. Most people don't realise that it's easy to let it slip back into an uncontrollable state. In this chapter, I will show you how to recognise the signs of relapse and be proactive in addressing them. Look forward to enjoying your recovery—but know that you carry a good insurance plan.

Discovering the Danger Zones

Let's take a look into the past, to the time when you first became unwell. This is important: it may give us clues to some of the warning signs that a relapse could be on the horizon.

> *Therapy Made A Difference—The Human Condition: A patient I was seeing, Pradeep, had first experienced anxiety at age fifteen. He had had a very upsetting family life. He came to me in his late thirties because he was tired of the health anxiety. Pradeep noticed upon reflection that the early warning signs of anxiety were the sensations of anxiety in his chest, which then led to him catatrophising and believing that he is going to die of cancer. This was the first step that led to him scaling back on social activities and stepping into the trap of only working and sleeping. Then, he would find that he felt tired and increased the number of hours he would spend sleeping, which of course left even less time available for socialisation. These habits eventually led to depression. Pradeep found a guided discovery technique useful, as he had been unaware of the signs pointing to a relapse. He targeted the health anxiety with experimentation and challenging his beliefs about certainty*

Do you know your danger zones? Do you know the signs of becoming un-well? Looking backwards will help you to look forwards with joy and eager anticipation for the future.

Signposting

Its important when coming to the end of your self discovery whether that be by yourself or with a therapist its important to look at the factors that lead to your illness in this episode. Checking out the Map can be very useful. Pradeep from the section above used a traffic light system. Red means stop and do immediately; amber is early warning that lets you know you need to address something now, before it becomes a red; and green is good to go. Look out for warning signs like brooding over unpleasant situations, worry thinking, and searching for "the why." Perhaps you also find yourself searching for perfection or losing touch with people around you. Another warning sign could be taking offense more readily than usual, and so on and so forth. Remember: your sign-posting may be different from others'. Vulnerabilities that you identify are like your Achilles' heel; the right conditions can make them worse and lead you back to anxiety.

Using Your Backup

Your backup system is your all-important social support network. Even the most antisocial amongst us need to have someone we can talk to on the other end of the phone. We are social creatures, and we learn partly from socialisation. Having a social network available can make recovering from anxiety a little easier.

It's important to address this as an investment for a return. If you burned all your bridges with friends and family during your last bout with anxiety, then make amends by taking a risk and making a call. Be sure to explain why you have been withdrawn and isolated. Do they understand your illness? If not, then help them to understand it a little bit. If you feel unsure about what you want or need from them, focus on what you don't want or need from them—a list will appear and you can use the opposites of things on that list to give you some ideas of what you *do* want or need. It's OK not to have all the answers—just try to explain that you have been struggling and feeling low, but that you have sought help via a GP, a psychiatrist, and a Mindfulness-Based Cognitive Therapist or CBT therapist. If you thought your therapist was helpful, then it is worthwhile maintaining contact with him or her.

Remembering That Practice, Practice, Practice Makes Permanent

Decide when you have completed your first eight-week run of mindfulness practice how you want to proceed. Try out all the meditations and practice exercises outlined here, then pick out the ones you liked best and establish them as part of your daily routine or weekly lifestyle. Consistency is key here—don't try to meditate on a schedule per se, because it puts pressure upon you to keep it, which usually is the first reason a new routine fails.

Being happy is about having a routine that works for you and your life right now.

Being Kind to Yourself

Research tells us that we are prone to be negative. With this in mind, it's worthwhile to remember that WE ARE WIRED for negativity. It's always going to be on the menu, whether you like it or not. In making adjustments, try to be kind to yourself by saying things like "Yep, there goes my mind again, trying to put me down!" Or try some sarcasm: "Thanks a lot, mind. That is really what I need right now...NOT!" Being kind does not cost anything and it's better than giving yourself a mental slap on the face. For those of you who struggle with generating positive thoughts and emotions, try as much as you can tolerate. Even if you tend to see everything as a double-edged sword, that's YOUR way forward, so it's OK as long as you don't go backwards and only generate destructive and negative thoughts and emotions.

Being in Charge

At this stage, you will have a good idea of what the issues and feelings that led to your anxiety were. You will have formed an idea about your maintaining factors and your vulnerabilities, too. Using the formulation form at the back of this book, try to reformulate your problem now. Has the issue changed—how? Look at the thoughts-feelings-behaviours cycle now and compare and contrast it with how it was in the beginning. Many clients like to see the changes and differences in order to give their self-esteem a boost. It's like a well-deserved treat.

The credit for your recovery is all down to you and all the work you put in. Its takes hard work to get to this stage and YOU have done it!! Be in the driver's seat—don't be a backseat driver where your health is concerned. Services and professionals are fallible, too, and can't provide a seamless service all the time. It's your responsibility to know what you want and to ask for it until someone gives it to you. Sometimes professionals don't act quickly enough, especially if a patient has "played down" his or her symptoms. Be clear in your communication and say, "I need help, my anxious thoughts have come back," and they will help you.

A Final Note: About Medication

Some people decide to just stop medication once their talking therapy concludes. PLEASE don't do that with out first talking with your GP or psychiatrist. The Maudsley Prescribing Guidelines says that once therapy has stopped, it's advisable to remain on medication for a further six months. This gives you time to put the therapy tool kit to work and to practice over and over. If you then want to stop medication, the GP or psychiatrist will discuss options with you. Remember: when coming off medication, there will be a bumpy landing. It takes the body time to adjust to the change. Many patients, however, choose to remain on medication for many years and this is OK, too.

Phase Four

FINISHING YOUR JOURNEY: REENERGISE ON SOME NOURISHING FACTS

CHAPTER 10

Ten Tips for Tackling Anxiety

In This Chapter You Will

- Learn how to build exercise into your life
- Develop the ability to say no to requests and people
- Commit to the moment

This chapter offers simple and succinct tips for tackling anxiety. Use it when you feel your concentration is particularly low. This is designed to be a quick read for you, and to put forwards ideas that can be put into practice immediately and change the way you are thinking almost immediately. These are also larger life skills that you can continue to practice and that will continue to yield benefits. Trying something new is a sure mood-booster. When you see that different results are to your liking, your quality of life will be enhanced. In this chapter, I will show you how important is to be in the driver's seat, how to draw the line, and how to live life to the fullest.

Enjoy Physical Exercise

Exercise is a good way of dusting off the cobwebs and "juggling the blood." When the blood is circulating slowly around the body, it needs a good shake to set off endorphins. When released, these help us to think clearly and to make a plan. It also raises the body's threshold for pain and changes the way you feel emotionally. It does not matter how light the exercise itself is—you just need to raise your heartbeat for twenty-five minutes. Exercise as often as you can. Look for simple ways to exercise, too. For instance, you could walk quickly up and down stairs, walk up the escalators at a tube station, get off the bus one stop early, turn the TV off one hour early or turn it on one hour later and go for a walk instead, lift dining room chairs like weights, clean floors, or even just pace and figeting. These are all good ways of increasing your fitness levels. If you able to do more, like running, swimming, or going to the gym, then go ahead—but don't overload your daily routine or put pressure on yourself about it. Another way to release endorphins is to listen to classical or instrumental music. Researchers have found that listening for thirty minutes can have the same effect on us as the muscle relaxant medication Valium.

Take Pride in Your Appearance

Many anxious people stop taking care of their appearance; when this goes, then pretty much all other activities go out of the window too since we worry about how we look to others. It is innate in us to want to look our best on dates or when meeting friends and family members. It's normal and enjoyable for us to preen when we are feeling good, but not when feeling low. Don't stick around waiting for external motivation—you will wait forever, and that's what anxiety feeds on. Try to encourage yourself to take care of your appearance regardless of how you feel. Have that shower, get a haircut, and get back into the swing of things. Makeup and hair are good focal points for bringing in the sense of "getting back to feeling like myself," but with a twist. The twist is that your way forward is going to include you looking better than you did before. Most clients have told me that their life is much better now than it was before the episode of anxiety; I would agree. Anxiety seems to be a thunderbolt that needed to happen in order to address someone's imbalanced life.

Take Care of Your Home

It does not matter that you cannot clean your house in one hour—let's drop the high expectations. Try doing a little bit every day; move through your home room by room. A tidy home can bring happiness. Remember: happiness leads to other positive things like welcoming visitors with some cake and a cup of tea. The home could lead to broadening your activities again because you might invite friends to meet there before venturing out to the village market, town, or city centre. Remember to keep yourself challenged with your chores but not overwhelmed.

Do Attention-Training Exercises

We looked earlier at learning to perform this useful skill that increases your ability to concentrate. The full version of the exercise lasts for fifteen minutes and includes focusing on nine sounds in succession. But to make it more achievable initially, focus on just three sounds for three minutes. Focus on an object in the room, then listen to the first sound one for a while before moving to sounds two and three. Then group the sounds together and listen to them that way for a moment or two before splitting them back off into the three individual sounds. Remember that if a sound disappears, you're supposed to find another sound—all the sounds need to be available in the present. You can also try this exercise without the visual focus—say when you're on the train, or at work making ginger tea.

Draw a Line in the Sand

It's an important life skill to be able to say no to requests. Learn to be able to draw a line in the sand—that is, tell others and yourself that there are lines that you prefer do not get crossed. Let's take the example of Rosa, who always takes on extra work for her colleagues and does most of the work at home to keep her family life running smoothly. Part of her anxiety stems from the fact that she is doing too much for others and has no self-interest. She gives off mixed signals. She wants to say no but she always smiles and gives in, which gives others the impression that she is fine with their requests. She suffers from I-Can't-Stand-It-Itis and does not want to sit with difficult feelings as she does not know how to manage them. Let's go for I-Can-Stand-It instead and learn to live with saying NO and negotiating your self-interestedness. It may mean tweaking your routines in order to help you be the best you can be. Knowing your limits is important to help you be the person that you want to be right now.

Be Assertive

Assertiveness means keeping the channels of communication open in order to negotiate. Keeping your walls of defense down is important in order to communicate effectively. Aggressiveness is the demanding stance taken when the possibility for negotiation has gone. In an effective negotiation, you have to entertain the possibility that you could lose the debate at hand—and accept this possibility with humility. An aggressive person will go to any lengths to stop the other party from winning.

Aggression is commonly divided into two types: direct and indirect. Direct aggression takes such forms as invading someone's personal space, verbally attacking another person with a raised voice, or physically attacking someone by using physical force. Indirect aggression includes back-biting, sarcasm, or using witty statements to put the other person down with the intention of harming them or avenging some perceived wrong. Passive aggression is a type of indirect aggression, and is typically characterised by the following: grumbling and making sacrifices that you want to be acknowledged—but in a form that others are supposed to guess. This approach is high-maintenance and drains the other party's energy quickly because the passive person has a lot of "rules" that others have to live by.

> *Top Tip: FAST*
> F *Fair to myself and others*
> A *No apologies for being alive*
> S *Stick to Ideas For Living (not do anything I'll regret later)*
> T *Be truthful, without excuses or exaggeration*

Make Attitudes Count

Flexible thinking allows us to be consistent with reality, helps us to achieve goals, and helps with cohesion in relationships. Attitudes can be changed in many ways, but one to mention here is activation. As an example, take

Joe: he is working towards having the attitude of "I prefer to have approval from others, but if I don't then this it's not catastrophic and life still goes on." This attitude is flexible and in keeping with the idea that you cannot get approval from everyone; it's just not achievable. The behaviours in line with this preferential attitude are: not overlooking signs of approval like smiles, gestures, and words like "I like" or "I love." Focus on a task rather than on the feeling of approval you're hoping to generate. Listening to what is actually said rather than on what you want to hear. Staying focused in the moment leads to long-term pleasure rather than living for the moment, which only creates short-term pleasure. Act as if you have successfully adopted the attitude you want for a week and then see if your mood is better or if it has resulted in any positive consequences.

Commit to Your Choices

"Being in the moment" is not an excuse for jumping from one thing to another. That would be "living for the moment," which is searching for pleasure all the time. That is not a sustainable way of living, and it ultimately leads to dissatisfaction and demoralisation. Being in the moment means focusing on a choice and following it through to the end, like making the choice to start a college course or making a surprise meal for your husband. It brings an authenticity to your life because it requires you to look, listen, feel, and be and thoughtful. It making you take steps to be true to yourself and others around you. People who are happier with themselves tend to have a daily structure and to be community focused; they look at the bigger picture of what they can contribute to others by joining a society or helping out with the local charity.

Know That Acceptance Is Not Resignation

Acceptance is another word for acknowledgment. To acknowledge our flaws does not mean that we must dwell on them too much. We see that they are there, but we focus on the positive. No one is perfect, and striving for perfection means missing out on one of the important messages in life: "ENJOY the good and WORK through the bad." Learning to accept ourselves, warts and all, and being kinder to ourselves when things go wrong increases our enjoyment of life, our resilience, and our well-being. It also helps us accept others as they are.

The Tourist Exercise

Think about a time when you visited a new country or place; so many things look brand-new. This is because curiosity plays a huge part in holding your focus and attention. Try this curiosity exercise on the way home from work or when collecting the children on the school run. Try to view your surroundings as if it was the first time you had ever seen them, then rate your mood before and afterwards. Invite your young children and teenagers do to this with you, too, and teach them a valuable lesson about perspective along the way—if you call it The Alien Exercise, they'll use their imaginations more and have fun doing it.

CHAPTER 11

Ten Mindful Attitudes for Easing Self-Critical Thoughts

In This Chapter You Will

- Discover that your weakness are actually your strengths
- Learn to take risks and allow yourself to be loved
- Recognise that creativity and innovation come from vulnerability

Rating oneself and measuring oneself—with negative results—is a habit that plagues us all. We are creatures of conditional acceptance. Every day, we make judgments about people because of economic or societal status, gender, sexual orientation, country of origin, and academic abilities, to name a few. We are wired to compare ourselves to others. Once the judgment has been made, we then evaluate them to see if they fit in with the groups of people we live, work and play with. But this often gets misunderstood and mixed in with the sense of self or as some call it, self-esteem. In this chapter I will show you a way forward, out of the common trappings caused by your anxiety. I will help you to step forward and be counted a human being who is equal to others. Remember: the mind is both your friend and your enemy. It gives you some clues as to how to react to any situation. With it sends you enemy information, learn to step back and observe the bigger picture as you find alternative ways to respond. Reacting to self-critical thoughts soon will be a thing of the past!

If I Look to the Future, Then I Have No Present

This statement is typical of absolute rigid perfectionists—they see the end result but take no enjoyment in the process of getting there. Enjoying the journey brings happiness, and living in the present moment means that you believe the future will arrive of its own volition and in its own good time. But ignoring the sensations we can find in the present means a reduction in joy. Structure will be lost and authenticity will run to zero because the people around you may tire of trying to connect with you. A disconnect like that then leads to dissatisfaction, which in turn leads people to see a demoralised you rather than your true personality, warts and all. The present is like pieces of a jigsaw puzzle that, when joined together, create a picture. This picture cannot be created overnight. We are human after all, and things tend to work out better when we don't try to overplan them or control them.

I Would Like Things to Be X, but Life Goes On If Not

There is nothing wrong with admitting that you want certain things:

- I want healthy children.
- I want a healthy life partner.
- I want a good income.

Keep wants phrased in rational statements like this, rather as irrational statements like "I *must* have X, and if I don't get it then life is over and I will be miserable!" One person's garbage is another's treasure, isn't it? So let's ditch hurtful and distressing comparisons and learn to be true to yourself and your family unit. Courage isn't present without fear, and some live a life that may seem soul-destroying to one person but workable and rewarding to others. This attitude is without conditions, making it workable and useful to live by. Placing conditions on your life just adds to the pain, so kick them to the curb!

Motto: Courage and fear are horns on the same goat, ride with it.

I Can Grow and Will Grow

Learning new things keeps life fresh, and is essential for happiness. Learning does not have to take the form of an academic qualification—it can mean simply connecting with others by letting a friend show you a new skill. This keeps your curiosity piqued and makes you engage with life. If you seek out new things to learn, you will develop in new and rewarding ways.

———

Pit Stop Exercise: Why not call a friend and ask for some help on a task? Or look through the papers for ways that you can impart your skills and knowledge to others?

———

It's not the fall that counts but what you do next. This is a most important attitude, as it will keep you motivated to brush yourself off after a failure or disappointment and try something else. If you were to stop after the first, second, or even thirty-first fall, no growth will happen. You will remain the same stagnant state—and this is not a great position for someone who is already anxious. As difficult as it may sound, just pick yourself up by focusing on the positive. It's human to try and try again.

———

Pit Stop Exercise: Instead of allowing your first words to yourself after a disappointment to be damning ones, try to tell yourself something positive like "I am not a failure yet" or "next time will be better."

———

Perfection Stifles Creativity

Perfectionist attitudes do not allow for vulnerability; therefore they do not allow for innovation. Vulnerability creates limits, and it's living through these brings about surprising innovations. To be perfect means there is nothing to test out or move forward for. Acknowledging that we are vulnerable means we accept that we can describe ourselves in many ways, and can develop ways to move forward with the help of others. If you build a wall around yourself but stop when it's only half-built, you can see who you are chatting with on the other side, but if the wall is built up to the ceiling then you cannot see anyone but yourself—life inside that wall is lonely, stifled, and creates a dearth of creativity.

It's OK to Get It Wrong—You're a Fallible Human Being

Get on with making some mistakes! Join the human race. Try not to rate yourself as being bad when you fail at something, try to view failures as individual incidents or actions that are bad. It may help to view yourself as a car that needs a door repaired—would you replace the whole car just to fix the door? Of course not! Then why do you damn yourself wholly for one mistake or even a series of mistakes? Just find a replacement door and move on. You are a beautiful human being—who makes mistakes.

It's Not the End of the World

Regardless of our personal dramas, the world will still go on tomorrow, next week, and so on. By allowing yourself to remain fixated on a moment from the past, you're making yourself suffer. Think of guilt as a ship that is anchored permanently at sea; you cannot pull up the anchor, so you are buffeted by storm after storm with no hope of escape. Letting go of guilt is a tough process, but it's important to know it that you will need to learn to let go of it before life gets better.

Pit Stop Exercise: When a negative emotion or guilty thought comes into your mind, say sarcastically "Thank you, mind, for trying to bring my mood down." Then get busy with living life.

I Can Find My Own Path to Fulfillment

Being an individual and living the life you were born to lead is the best way forward. Whether you are gay, lesbian, Afro-Caribbean, African, French, Tamil, Sinhalese, adopted, fostered, male, female, employed, unemployed, a student, a teacher, Christian, Muslim, a gay dad, a lesbian mother, transsexual, a transvestite, middle class, working class, upper-middle class, a Tory supporter, or a Labour supporter, live the life you want to lead. It's about being proud to be who you are and having the humility to move forward. Be able to shout to the silver of the moon "I am what I am and I am glad for it!" We should not need to put anyone else down, we should be focusing on own journeys and helping others along theirs. No one has the right to judge, but let's accept that judgment is all around: in the media, with friends, and from Joe Bloggs! This is what humans do, so we must learn to live life with it.

Pit Stop Exercise: Imagine that a radio is playing in the background. The noise is low—it's just background music—so you don't really even notice it until your favourite tune comes on. Suddenly, it sounds louder to you even though the volume has not been altered. This is because your attention is focused on it. You end up singing along with it. This is what it is like with judgments made by yourself and others—focusing on them makes them louder. Try using the environment around you to distract you from them. Try focusing on the task you were engaged in before the intrusive or hurtful thought came by. Then rate your mood before and after to measure the effect of your behaviour choice. Determine within yourself if this is a useful exercise to try again another time.

It's OK to Love and Be Loved

Allowing ourselves to be loved is a life-changing experience. We must risk so much to try it, and in return we change so much. But if life has dealt you a heavy blow once, the tendency is to close up and to try and stop hurt from entering our lives again. But who loses out? Ultimately it's you and your close friends and family, because the authenticity has gone from your relationships.

Playing over hurtful old stories in the mind drains you of energy, which causes you to cancel plans. Or that behaviour allows people to catch you off-guard, making it more likely that you'll respond to them is an aggressive or worried manner; this will lead people to believe that you are a tortured soul and unpleasant to be around. Human nature being what it is, we make assumptions and hold those assumptions for a while when we see a pattern of behaviour emerging. Judgments like "she is bitter and twisted" or "Billy no mates" are commonly used to describe someone who is closed off and will not allow others to love them—or indeed allow themselves to love another. There is no simple way to force yourself to open up to others, but the door to your heart has to be opened to allow in some fresh air from time to time. New perspectives and fresh experiences give it life and energy. Who said that your heart should never get broken? Who promised that? A life with brokenness is life that is vibrant, authentic, renewed, and full of new opportunities like writing a book, retraining, extending your family, taking a promotion, inventing something, being innovative, or allowing a new lover to walk in.

Remember: Don't underestimate yourself. Surprising yourself is the best way to live!

No One Person Has the Full Truth, so Let's Join Forces

Nelson Mandela believed this to be true. And it works if we allow it to work. No one person, group, politician, organised religion, spiritual guide, sexual orientation, or race has the full truth about the human experience. But each knows a part of the truth. When we unite in our diversity, we form true unity. Join forces with friends, family, and other members of your social network—they will have knowledge that may be useful to you, or they may have an attitude towards life that is attractive to you. You may want to try out or experiment with ways other people approach life. Let's not be quick to exclude others; we are all are finding our way through life. By giving them a chance you might have gained your own lifeline.

———•———

Pit Stop Exercise: Use community-based activities to introduce yourself to others, like Halloween trick-or-treating, Christmas carolling, volunteering with Scouts/Brownies, visiting local markets, selling produce, mentoring a student, or making your skills available to the community. This can lead to meeting up for a coffee with a new acquaintance at first and then possibly to more meaningful interactions in the future.

———•———

It Is In Our Diversity That We Have Our Unity

We are not all the same and thank God as this would make life boring. Each will have their own problem and ways of coping. They also may find an answer that you never thought about and hence the community of mankind comes together to help. Lets reach out to others who you would never dream of talking to and see what difference you can make in another persons life. Can the observant Muslim man speak to a gay person and enjoy their company? Can a city man spend time with a homeless man and buy him soup? It is this diversity that gives us a strength, which many in terrorist organisations would seek to hinder and destroy

CHAPTER 12

Ten Mindful Resources for Managing Anxiety

In This Chapter You Will

- ◆ Use ordinary, everyday things to lift your mood
- ◆ See how growth can help in journeying out from anxiety and continued wellness
- ◆ Look at how helping others can help you get better

The positive psychology camp has been researching the secrets of happiness for years. It basically boils down to how well we relate to others and society. Forgiveness, letting go, engaging, having fun, and a side salad of acceptance are the keys to happiness. Notice that success was not listed among the prerequisites for happiness; happiness, however, may lead to success. As we are social beings, this makes a lot of sense. Why not try to reach out and see what changes you can make by following the steps outlined in this chapter? I will show you how to use skills like letting go, allowing, and using wisdom to make the right choices.

Doing the Chocolate Twirl Bite Size Chunk
This is a good exercise for slowing down. There is no better way than to focus on one of the smallest food items—the chocolate chunk. Take a chocolate chunk and hold it between your fingers. Roll it around. Describing what

you feel—its texture and whether that reminds you of anything else. This is a simple skill that many of us don't practice. Then move it under your nose and describe what you smell. Do you notice any sensations in your body? Maybe you notice that you are beginning to salivate or you have hunger pains. Maybe it causes a memory to surface in the present of a past experience, like baking cakes or your mother's cooking. Teasing the senses a little bit more by holding off on eating the chocolate chunk for a while longer. Then place the whole chocolate chunk on your tongue and leave it there for a while. Describe what is happening now. Hold off swallowing a little longer to again tease your senses some more. As the chocolate chunk begins to crumble on the tongue resist any movement and wait a little longer. Then a long period of time would have been spent here and then when all the sensations are going crazy then move the tongue and begin to eat—why? To obtain a perspective that is different from just gulping down food within a few moments without engaging your senses in the experience. Rushing from one thing to another without experiencing anything seems pointless. This mirrors the experience of a problem called stress.

Diagnosis Corner: Stress
The human body is designed to use stress for positive reasons, such as getting tasks done and feeling a sense of achievement for having challenged ourselves. When combined with rewards and down time, stress can be a positive force in our lives. Stress becomes negative force when a person faces continuous challenges without relief or relaxation. As a result, the person becomes overworked and stress-related tension builds, leading to chronic stress or to depression-related symptoms.

Engaging in the Walking Meditation

Try walking slowly, with no other aim than taking in the view. Look for birds, bees, the sound of twigs crunching under your shoes, and the wind on your cheeks. Focus your attention on simple things that exist in the present moment. Be curious about colours, textures, and the taste of blackberries growing wild by the side of the road. Use your environment to get back in touch with your senses.

Diagnosis Corner: Biodiversity
This term is used by scientists to refer to the good bacteria that helps us to be healthy, strong individuals. Scientists have found that people with allergies have low levels of good bacteria. These people also tend not to wander very far from home. Research is still ongoing, but the evidence to date suggests that venturing out and going for walks in the woods, parks, and beaches and playing in the environment in general by getting our hands dirty is good for us because it exposes us to many different types of beneficial bacteria. Eating berries on a walk also exposes us to good bacteria.

Brushing Your Teeth

One of your most mundane daily activities can help you slow it right down and pay attention to small sensations in a meaningful way: brushing your teeth. If you occasionally stop to pay attention to each stroke and sensation, it will help you live in the moment and will remind you not to go through your day on autopilot. Other activities that provide similar opportunities include: washing the body, drying the body, flossing teeth, washing hair, drying hair, washing your face, cleansing your face, lotioning your body, applying makeup, etc. Choose one activity per week to focus on and then describe what you notice when you do, but without judgment. If you find yourself making a judgment, take a mental note of it and then, with a kindly attitude, bring your attention back to the activity at hand.

Noticing the Pleasure in the Small Stuff

There are so many things to notice—butterflies, birds, and trees. There are probably also people around you who you have not noticed in a while. They would probably appreciate some of your attention, too. Maybe they have changed without your noticing. Did you miss one of your baby's developmental milestones, or its first, second, or even forty-fourth word said? Get in touch with your environment and yourself by paying attention to the small things of everyday life and learn to sit quietly with the feelings they bring.

Keeping in Touch

We know that our relationships with other people are the most impor-tant component of happiness. People with strong relationships are happier, healthier, and live longer. Our close relationships with family and friends provide love, meaning, and support and increase our feelings of self-worth. Our broader social networks bring us a sense of belonging. So it's vital that we take actions to strengthen our relationships and make new connections.

Making Someone Else Happy

Caring about others is fundamental to our happiness. Helping other peo-ple is not only good for them, it's good for us, too. It makes us happier and can help to improve our health. Giving also creates stronger connections between people and helps to build a happier society for everyone. Giving is not all about money—we can also give our time, ideas, and energy. If you want to feel good, do good.

Offering Forgiveness

Forgiving people helps to mend relationships with others and yourself, and it also helps us to move forward and experience happiness. It might not seem like it makes logical sense sometimes to forgive someone for saying a sinful word or for taking hurtful action against you, but it does unblock your life in ways that people find almost indescribable. They are able to be happy again and to move forward in their life.

Allowing

Trying to control things that cannot be controlled is exhausting. Unpleasant emotions are invariably accompanied by parallel sensations in the body. If we gently, willingly focus our attention right into these areas of intense sensation and discomfort, we bring about both immediate and longer-term effects. We immediately short-circuit any unhelpful avoidance tendencies our minds might be creating. We also disrupt the automatic links among body sensations, feelings, and thoughts that perpetuate vicious cycles, fuel anxiety, and initiate downward mood spirals. In the longer run, we develop more skillful ways of being in a relationship with uncomfortable experiences. Rather than seeing them as "bad and threatening things," a view that triggers avoidance and gets us stuck in suffering, we begin to see unpleasant experiences for what they are: passing events. The way we remember events boils down to bundles of bodily sensations, feelings, and thoughts. Greet them with a sense of interest and curiosity as best you can, rather than with a sense of unease, hatred, and dread. Welcome them in—they are already here anyway.

Fostering Appreciation

Be thankful and take stock of the work that you have achieved. Reflection is a useful first exercise for making links as you learn to develop insight. It gives you options to work on. Appreciation is the empathy you develop—it's like giving yourself a warm pat on the back, or a hug that says, "Everything is good with the work you have done." It's vital to do this—awareness that helps us to be healthy and happy. Give it a go!

Establishing Your Relationship with Yourself

Nobody's perfect. The most important person is you. Make a start at developing a relationship with yourself today by getting to know your emotional likes and dislikes. So often we compare a negative view of ourselves with an unrealistic view of other people. Dwelling on our flaws—what we're not rather than what we are—makes it much harder to be happy. Learn to accept yourself, warts and all, and be kind to yourself when things go wrong. This effort will increase your enjoyment of life, your resilience, and your well-being. It also helps you accept others as they are.

CHAPTER 13

Ten Tips for Challenging Distorted Thinking

In This Chapter You Will

- Learn which thoughts are OK to skip over
- Learn to carry out a stop-and-search on your thoughts
- Learn to step back and view thoughts as if from a distance

Many different thinking styles fuel anxiety. In previous chapters, we have looked at viewing thoughts as mental events that contain a definite thought-feeling connection. For instance, when you have thoughts of escape, that means anxiety is present; your coping behaviour is to stand close to a door. In this chapter, I will be reviewing some of the thinking styles that appear with anxiety so that you can learn to notice them and label them to aide you in making decisions. Remember that observation is the key to understanding what these thinking styles do at the moment when you think them. If you know how the enemy acts, then you are miles ahead and can stop it in its tracks!

Avoid Catastrophising

Dr Aaron Beck MD called "catastrophising" the mind's ability to create a tempest in a teapot or to make mountains out of molehills. Catastrophic thinking is an exaggeration of a perceived threat with 2 types of catastrophe.

a) Probability Distortion: Exaggerating the chances of a negative experience occurring, e.g. "I know they won't like me."

b) Severity Distortion: Exaggerating the consequences of what would happen if the negative experience did occur. It's believing a merely "bad" outcome would be truly "awful" or "terrible."

Top Tip: Try tweaking an awful statement by adding "yet" or "but" to it. For instance, "I know they won't like me—yet—as I have only started my first lesson." Or "It is really bad—but—let's see what happens next." In this way, you are tapping into the reality of the situation rather than allowing yourself to get carried away with negativity. Reality always offers more positive ideas for living.

Step into the Grey

The irrational thinking is often called black-and-white thinking or all-or-nothing thinking. When we think irrationally, things are polarised into either/or extremes. There is no middle ground. For example, you might tell yourself "Either I am a success at this, or I am a total failure," or "I will either do things perfectly or it's a complete waste of time." These thought patterns drain energy and are limiting because they create a boxed-in effect on your life.

Top Tip: Step into the grey by looking to the middle ground. "I did not succeed at passing my exam today, but it does not mean I am a failure at life. I can sit the exam again. Life goes on."

Keep the Dictator in His Place

Think of intrusive, unwanted thoughts that pile in and tell you that you are a bad person if you don't clean your house, or if you don't move items into a pattern to make them symmetrical with all the other objects on a table as a dictator. It's the "coulda, shoulda, woulda" thinking that is so rigid it won't let you or others off the hook. Psychoanalysts call this mafioso thinking.

Top Tip: Try standing up to the dictator by being democratic with your thoughts. Rules can be broken.

Think Practically—Not Magically

Have you ever used magical thinking for good? It is always associated with the bad, i.e. "If I saw that, then I am bad," or "If I don't check every door then my house will get robbed and my family will be killed." These are upsetting, intrusive, unwanted thoughts. They that can plague us through illnesses like depression and anxiety disorders. This is what CBT Psychotherapists call Thought Action Fusion (TAF)—I think it therefore it is true. But let's put it to the test with positive things, like winning the lotto. How many of us have bought a ticket tried with all our might to apply TAF? We all believe when buy the ticket, that ours will be the winner. Does our wanting it to be true make it come true? If it did work, then we would all get a penny each, not a jackpot of millions, so why believe it for the bad thoughts?

Try instead to act like a scientist experimenting with those Thought Action Fusion/magical thoughts and see what happens. Instead of constantly checking for instance: if all the light sockets are off all the time, reduce the number as much as you can and see what happens to your memory. Constant checking does lead to more checking, because it does not improve confidence or the ability to remember. It only reduces confidence—hence you do it more. Try checking less and comparing previous experiences with the now more.

Don't Police Every Thought

The problem with intrusive and unwanted thoughts is that we learn that we must become vigilant and stand guard to block them out. The problem with blocking is that one thought splits into twenty thoughts, then forty, etc. It's more practical to deal with them as they present originally.

———

Pit Stop Exercise: Try imaging a pink fluffy elephant and look at its features for a while. Now STOP thinking about the pink elephant and what happens? You will find that many pink elephants are popping in automatically. This is what the mind does when you attempt to block unwanted intrusive thoughts

But this means allowing the thought in the first place! Policing thoughts is exhausting. You spend so much energy on it that it causes you to miss out on living the life you want to lead. Policing means your focus is on barricading the door against possible gate-crashers and not on the party behind you. Try instead to focus upon the direction you want to or need to take. The focus then becomes practical, and if carried out in the right spirit, you will not have time to police all your thoughts anyway!

Party Like It's 1999!

Imagine the best party in the world. It's YOU—and who you spend time with and the activities you do. A problem with policing thoughts is that your back is all that your guests see because you're too busy peeking out the door. They don't see your face, so they can't communicate with you because you are heavily preoccupied with damaging stuff. Try instead to focus on behaviours and attitudes that will lead to you turning around and walking towards the chair in the centre of the room where all your guests are waiting to spend time with you.

Don't Take Things Personally

Overreacting to things is not good for your heart—it will get broken many times over if you take things personally all the time. Negative events from your past can leave a sensitive mark on your soul, which can lead to overreacting to situations in the here and now. Try asking yourself these questions to develop a different view: Is my reaction disproportionate to the sin committed? Is my past catching up with me? Is my reaction consistent with where I want this relationship to eventually lead in the future? Is this the right time to argue about this? Sometimes you have to choose your battles. If you try to fight every time someone offends you—intentionally or not—then others will perceive you as a wailing, loud piece of noise and will try to avoid you in the future.

Consider Possibilities

When you start to get caught up with intrusive thoughts, you can quickly start to develop feelings of unhealthy anger or unhealthy anxiety. Suddenly, it becomes difficult to see the wood for the trees. This makes it easy for us to get caught up in the one option that leads to a downward-spiralling mood. And that in turn leads to a higher probability of carrying out more self-defeating behaviours. Instead step away, pause, and take a breath. Focus on the belly and its movement and even if your mind wanders onto other things, just move your focus back to the belly. Try to make this meditation last for five minutes or more. Getting calm will help you see not just one rigid option dictated by anger, but two or more other options that may be more helpful to you and that can lead you away from the spiralling, self-defeating behaviours.

Know That You're Fallible

Look at what you can do rather than what you can't. We are not super-men and women—give up trying to make yourself appear as the best all the time, in all situations, to all people. You are allowed to make mistakes. Take a breath. If you are usually a stickler for ironing, try walking around in a wrinkled shirt for a day. If you are usually a stickler for punctuality, arrive late to an appointment. Try focusing on yourself and your loved ones and try to see the enjoyment that the important people around you can bring.

Remember That Shouting at It Does Not Get Rid of It

Losing your temper does not mean you get rid of whatever was bothering you. It just adds more weight, because it leads you to brood about how you have upset others. If you have an anger problem, try the anger four-step exercise in Chapter 5. Also try this problem-solving technique: Write down in one sentence what the problem is, and then, in one sentence, what the solution is. Remember not to write a long essay about many problems. Turn each problem into a one-act play! This approach can cut through the smoke and bring about focused action.

REFERENCES OF READING MATERIAL

1. Addis,. Martell, C, & Jacobson, N. (2001) Depression in Context. Norton Professional Books
   Beck, A.T. (1970). *Depression causes and treatment*. Philadelphia: University of Pennsylvania Press.

2. Beck, A.T. (1976). *Cognitive therapy and the emotional disorders*. New York: International Universities Press

3. Beck, A., Rush, A., Shaw, B., & Emery, G. (1979). *Cognitive therapy of depression*. Guildford, New York

4. Bennett-Levy, J., Butler, G., Fennell, M., Hackmann, A., Meullar, M., & Westbrooke, D. (2004) *Oxford guide to behavioural experiments in cognitive therapy*. Oxford University Press, Oxford

5. Biglan, A. (1993) Capturing Skinner's legacy to behaviour therapy. *Behaviour Therapist*, 16, 3-5

6. Carver, C.S. & Scheier, M.F (2001) On the structure of behavioural self-regulation. In M.Boekaets, P. R.Pintrich & M. Zeidner (Eds), *Handbook of Self regulation: Theory, research, applications*. San Diago: Academic Press.

7. Chamberlain, J.M & Haaga, D.A.F. (2001a) Unconditional self acceptance and psychological health. *Journal of Rational Emotive and Cognitive Behaviour Therapy*, **19 (3),** 163-176.

8. Chamberlain, J.M & Haaga, D.A.F. (2001b) Unconditional self acceptance and responses to negative feedback. *Journal of Rational Emotive and Cognitive Behaviour Therapy*, **19 (3),** 177-189.

9. Deeks, A.A & McCabe, M.P. (2004) Well-being and menopause: An investigation of purpose in life, self-acceptance and social role in

premenopausal, perimenopausal and postmenopausal women. *Quality of Life*. **13**, 389-398.

10. Dryden, W. (Ed). (2003) *Rational Emotive Behaviour Therapy: theoretical developments.* Brunner-Routledge

11. Ellis, A. E. (1962) *Reason and Emotion in Psychotherapy.* New Jersey, The Citadel Press

12. Flett, G.L., Besser, A., Davis, R.A & Hewitt, P.L. (2003) Dimensions of perfectionism, unconditional self acceptance, and depression. *Journal of Rational Emotive and Cognitive Behaviour Therapy* **21(2)**, 119-138.

13. Gilbert, P (2009) Compassionate Mind. Constable

14. Houser, R. (1998). *Counselling and Educational Research.* Sage

15. Greenberger, D. & Padsesky, C.A. (1995). *Mind over mood. A cognitive therapy treatment manual for clients.* New York: Guildford Press.

16. Haaga, D.A.F., Dryden, W. & Dancey, C.P. (1991) Measurement of Rational Emotive Therapy in outcome studies. *Journal of Rational Emotive and Cognitive Behaviour Therapy*, 9(2), 73-87

17. Haaga, A. F., & Davison, G. C. (1993). An appraisal of rational-emotive therapy. *Journal of Consulting and Clinical Psychology*, 61, 215-220

18. Harrison, Y., Horne, J.A. (1999) One night of sleep loss impairs innovative thinking and flexible decision making. *Organizational Behavior and Human Decision Processes*, 78, 128-145.

19. Hawton, K., Salkovskis, P.M., Kirk, J., Clark, D.M (Eds) (1989). *Cognitive behaviour therapy for psychiatric problems: A practical guide.* Oxford University Press, Oxford.

20. Hayes, S. C., & Hayes, L. J. (1992) Some clinical implications of contextualist behaviourism: The example of cognition. *Behaviour Therapy*, 23, 225-250

21. James, W. (1980). *Principles of psychology*. New York: Holt

22. Kanfer, F. H.,(1975). *Self- management methods*. In F.H Kanfer & A.P Goldstein (Eds). Helping people change: A textbook of methods (pp. 334-389). New York: Pergamon Press.

23. Kanfer, F.H., & Stevenson, M.K. (1985). The effects of self-regulation on concurrent cognitive processing. *Cognitive Therapy and Research*, 9, 667-684.

24. Kazdin, A.E. (1986) Comparative outcome studies of psychotherapy: Methodological issues and strategies. *Journal of Consulting and Clinical Psychology*, 54, 95-105.

25. Loftus, E. F. (2004). Memories of things unknown. *Current Directions in Psychological Science*, 13, 145-147

26. Meichenbaum, D. (1985*). Stress inoculation training*. New York: Pergamon Press.

27. Mischel, W., & Shoda, Y. (1995). A cognitive affective system theory of personality: Reconceptualizing situations, dispositions, dynamics and invariences in personality structure. *Psychological Review*, 102, 246-268.

28. Novaco, R.W. (1976). Anger Conrol: *The Development and Evaluation of an Experimental Treatment*. Lexington Mass: Lexington Books.

29. Novaco, R.W. (1977) Stress inoculation: a cognitive therapy for anger and its application to a case of depression. *Journal of Consulting and Clinical Psychology* 44: 681.

30. Ozer, E.M. & Bandura, A. (1990). Mechanisms governing empowerment effects: A self efficacy analysis. *Journal of Personality and Social Psychology*, 58, 472-486.

31. Proschaska, J.O., & DiClemente, C.C. (1992). Stages of change in the modification of problem behaviours. In M. Herzen, R.M Eisler &P.M Miller (Eds), *Progress in behaviour modification* (Vol. 28), pp 183-218. Sycamore, Il. Sycamore Publishing Company

32. Ross, M., & Conway, M.(1986). *Remembering one's own past. The construction of personal histories.* In R.M. Sorrentino & E.T. Higgings (Eds)., Handbook of motivation and cognition (pp. 130-150). New York: The Guildford Press.

33. Russell, J. (1996). *Agency: Its role in mental development.* Hove: Erlbaum (UK), Taylor & Francis

34. Simmons, J., & Griffiths, R. (2009) *CBT for Beginners.* London Sage Publication Ltd.

35. Skinner, B. F. (1971) *Beyond freedom and dignity.* New York: Knopf

36. Spinoza, B. de (1677). *Ethics*, translate. A Boyle, 1959, London: Dent.

37. Strupp, HH (1978) Psychotherapy research and practice – an overview. In AE Bergin & SL Garfield (Eds.), <u>Handbook of psychotherapy and behavior change</u> (2nd ed.), New York: Wiley.

38. Walters, G. D. (2000). Behavioral self-control training for problem drinkers: a meta-analysis of randomized control studies. *Behavior Therapy*, 31, 135–149.

39. Watson, D.W., & Tharp, G. (2007). *Self –directed behaviour* (9th Ed) Thompson Wadsworth

40. Wolpe, J. (1958). <u>Psychotherapy by reciprocal inhibition</u>. Stanford: Stanford University Press

Appendices

Behaviour Activation Form

Behaviour Activation Form

	Rate mood before activity	Pleasure activity	Rate mood after activity	Rate mood before chore activity	Chore Activity	Rate mood after activity
Example	0/10	Going to feed the ducks	7/10	0/10	Washing the dog	7/10
Sunday						
Monday						
Tuesday						
Wednesday						
Thursday						
Friday						
Saturday						

Cost-Benefit Analysis

Cost Benefit Analysis blank form in appendices

ADVANTAGES/BENEFITS OF ....

SHORT TERM – for yourself
1
2
3
4
5
6

SHORT TERM – for other people
1
2
3
4
5
6

LONG TERM – for yourself
1 ....
2 ....
3 ....
4 ....
5 ....
6 ....

LONG TERM – for other people
1 ....
2 ....
3 ....
4 ....
5 ....
6 ....

DISADVANTAGES/BENEFITS OF ....

SHORT TERM – for yourself
1
2
3
4
5
6

SHORT TERM – for other people
1
2
3
4
5
6

LONG TERM – for yourself
1 ....
2 ....
3 ....
4 ....
5 ....
6 ....

LONG TERM – for other people
1 ....
2 ....
3 ....
4 ....
5 ....
6 ....

Formulation of my Beliefs and Rules

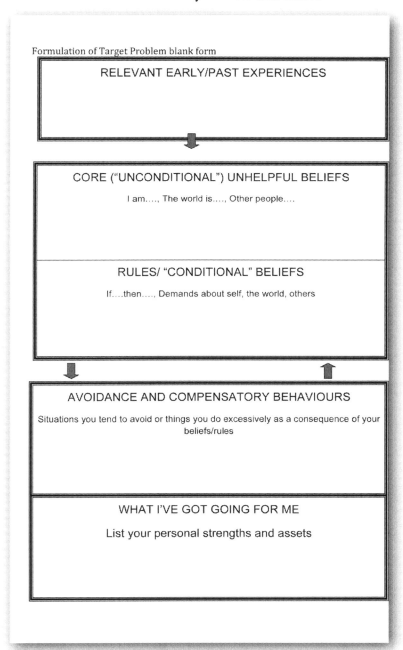

Formulation of Target Problem blank form

RELEVANT EARLY/PAST EXPERIENCES

CORE ("UNCONDITIONAL") UNHELPFUL BELIEFS

I am...., The world is...., Other people....

RULES/ "CONDITIONAL" BELIEFS

If....then...., Demands about self, the world, others

AVOIDANCE AND COMPENSATORY BEHAVIOURS

Situations you tend to avoid or things you do excessively as a consequence of your beliefs/rules

WHAT I'VE GOT GOING FOR ME

List your personal strengths and assets

Ideas for Living Form

Ideas For Living Form in appendices

Intimacy- Do you want to be a warm, giving, authentic, genuine, forgiving, caring, trustworthy, self accepting person	**Spirituality**-Are you involved in organized religion or just spiritual spending moments by yourself? If so have you let this lapse and need to discover again your spirituality?
Social-Do you want to be community focused, volunteering, providing parties, life and soul of party, thoughtful, caring person	**Politics**-Do you believe passionately but now don't bother? Are you a libertarian, Tory, Liberal, or labour voter?
Mental Health-Do you want to be proud of being a person who shares about how they feel, their thoughts, actions and that being vulnerable is a sign of strength and good mental health	**Parenthood**-Do you want to be caring, shy, outrageous, cool, pedantic, easy going, generous, cautious, colourful, intelligent, creative, stern, disciplinarian etc

Ideas for Living form part 2

Leisure-Do you want to be active in sports, reading, swimming, cooking, interpretation, art, movie watching, debating, riding, cycling, rambling etc	**Work**-What type of worker do you want to be? Warm, easy going, strict, earnest, patient, kind, log suffering, energetic, autonomous, allowing delegation, permitting attitude etc
Sexuality-Are you wanting to be the best gay, lesbian, bisexual, transgendered, transvestite, curious person who likes to define their sexuality by different ways rather than living to other expectations?	**Ethnicity/Culture**-Do you hide away from the person you were born to be? Instead is it time to be proud and find ways from your ethnicity/Culture that can help relax you and bring energy into your life.
Gender-What kind of man or woman do you want to be? Is it a strong minded, intellectual, fun, bubbly, serious, thoughtful, energetic, passive, peaceful etc	**Genetic**- (This is about those who have been adopted). Do you want to lead a life that your parents have helped create for you or do you want to capture something from your birth parents? Do you want to be remembered as being from a certain back ground, ethnicity, Culture, country, language etc

Positive Data Form

Positive Data Form in appendices

Date	Comments

Practice of Meditation Form

Practice of Meditation form in appendices

Date	Comments

Index

A.

Anger 61
Anger 4-step 62
Anxiety 63
Appearance 101
Appetite 29
Artist 40
Assertive 113
Autonomous Depression 17
Autopilot 38
Awareness 49, 102
B.
Bodily Distress 99
Brain 46
Breath 42, 43, 46, 48
Brooding 57
Business owner 40
C.
Cancer 99
Change 69
Compassion 57, 72
Concentration 31, 38
Concentration, back on track 34
Control 38

Cost-Benefit Analysis 83

Creativity 48

D.

Decisions 51, 52

Depression—What fuels it? 19, 20, 21, 23, 29, 48, 53

Describing 60

Diabetes 98

Diagnosis Corner 47, 90, 108

Doctors 85

E.

Emotions 25, 26, 27, 53, 59, 60, 67

Emotional Responsibility 28

Exercise 98, 99

F.

Fact Corner 34, 40

Flexibility 44

Formulation 73

Forgiveness 122

G.

Gay 40, 55

H.

Happiness 108,109,110

High Frustration Tolerance 74

High Self-Esteem 65

Heart 99

Heart (High Blood Pressure) 88

Hurt 64

Husband 39

I.

Ideas for Living 21, 22, 23, 39

Intruders 48

Intuition 51

Irrational beliefs 26

Irritability 32

Isolation 33

J.
Jealousy 24
K.
Kindness 79,109
L.
Lacking pleasure 28
Life-Shrinkage 41
Listening 62
Long-Term Conditions 98, 99,100
Low Frustration Tolerance 74
Low Mood 32
M.
Meditations 46
Mindfulness 35, 52, 71, 89, 95, 103, 121
Mindfulness, Beginner Mind 35, 44
Moments 49
Mood Chart 28
Motto 44, 54, 55, 58, 75
Multiple Sclerosis 100
N.
Noticing 67
O.
Obsessions 48
Off-Duty Time 91
P.
Pain 70, 101
Parent 40
Pause 54
Personality 44
Pit Stop Exercises 36, 64, 71, 78, 81, 92, 95, 102
Pleasure, lack of 28
Pleasure, increase in 25
Positive data 79
Professionals 96, 97
Prejudice Model 81, 82

Problem-Solving 68
Psychobabble Defined 83
R.
Raisin 107
Rational Emotive Imagery 90
Reasoning 47
Relapse 107,108,109
Relationships 19, 20, 35, 80, 91
Remember 105
S.
Safety-Seeking Behaviours 57
Self-Affirming Statements 37
Self-Esteem 73, 74, 75, 76, 77
Self-Harming 33
Saying no 92
Sex changes 33
Shame 60, 61
Sociotropic Depression 17
Stress 68, 103, 104, 105
Strokes 99
Strokes (TIA)
Suicide 34
System 46, 47
T.
Task Confidence 86
Thinking 44, 45, 54, 55, 57, 69, 80, 90, 91, 92, 101, 102, 113, 115, 116, 117, 118, 119
Thought Action Fusion 50
Top Tip 27, 86
Tourist Exercise 114
TRAP/TRAC 56, 93
U.
Unconditional Self-Acceptance 78, 84, 85, 86, 114
Unconditional Other-Acceptance 79
Unconditional Life-Acceptance 79

V.
Void, filling with junk 31
Vulnerability 44
W.
Warehouse 53
Wife 35
Worker 39
Worry 57

Printed in Great Britain
by Amazon